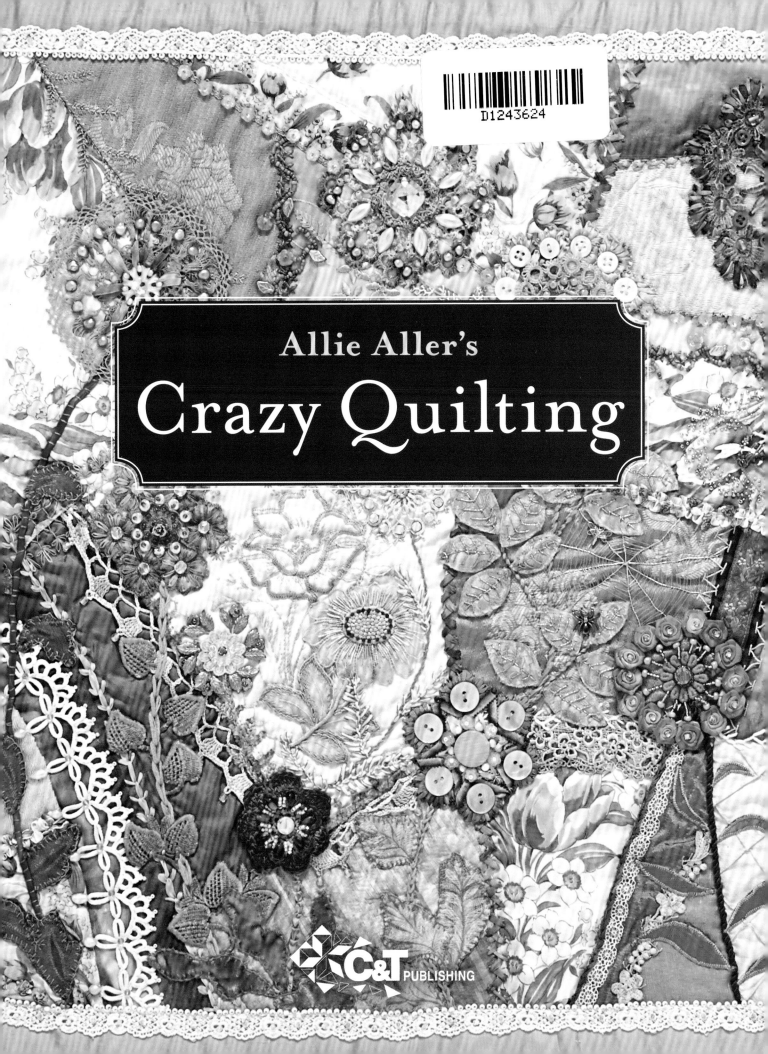

Allie Aller's
Crazy Quilting

C&T PUBLISHING

Text copyright © 2011 by Allison Ann Aller

Artwork copyright © 2011 by C&T Publishing, Inc.

Publisher: Amy Marson

Creative Director: Gailen Runge

Acquisitions Editor: Susanne Woods

Editor: Cynthia Bix

Technical Editors: Sandy Peterson and Teresa Stroin

Cover/Book Designer: Kerry Graham

Production Coordinator: Kirstie L. Pettersen

Production Editor: Alice Mace Nakanishi

Illustrator: Mary Flynn

Photography by Christina Carty-Francis and Diane Pedersen
of C&T Publishing, Inc., unless otherwise noted; step-by-step
photography by Allison Ann Aller in the chapter Work in Progress:
A Crazy Quilt from Start to Finish.

Published by C&T Publishing, Inc., P.O. Box 1456, Lafayette, CA 94549

Library of Congress Cataloging-in-Publication Data

Aller, Allison Ann, 1954-

Allie Aller's crazy quilting : modern piecing & embellishing techniques
for joyful stitching / Allison Ann Aller.

p. cm.

ISBN 978-1-60705-173-2 (softcover)

1. Crazy quilts. 2. Patchwork--Patterns. 3. Quilting--Patterns. I. Title. II.
Title: Crazy quilting.

TT835.A457 2011

746.46--dc22

2010024416

Printed in China

10 9 8 7

Contents

Dedication

Nancy, Class of '44–'45, 8" × 10",
by the author, 2007

To Mom
I will always miss you and love you.

Acknowledgments

My fellow quilters have inspired me for decades, but except for an incomparable annual quilters' retreat at Point Bonita, I had always sewed by myself out here in the country—until the advent of blogging. That's when I found my stitching cyber-circle of friends, which now stretches all around the world. Our exchange of ideas and warm support is hugely fulfilling. I can't name everyone whom I've grown to love and admire in the online textile community, but you are all very special to me, and I thank you with all my heart for your inspiration, support, and great company.

For many years, www.cqmagonline.com has been a terrific (and free) online resource for crazy quilters, and I would like to thank the hardworking staff for all their efforts. I have loved being a member of the team, too.

I hope the "guest stitchers" who have kindly allowed me to share their work here will know how much I appreciate them: Jo Newsham, Susan Elliott, Betty Pillsbury, Sharon Boggon, Martha Green, Marty Trahan, Barbara Curiel, Debra Spincic, and Deb Hardman.

Thanks to Maureen Greeson for her inspiration! My gratitude goes to Judie Bellingham of www.bellaonline.com for her design wall idea.

Catherine Smith, of Newberg, Oregon, gave me the machine-embroidered Angelina butterflies and Debra Spincic, of Montgomery, Texas, the beautiful hummingbirds for my *Crazy in the Garden* quilt (next page). The quilt would not be the same without them!

Without the interest and guidance of my agent, Courtney Miller-Callahan, this book would never have happened. My editors, Cynthia Bix and Sandy Peterson, held my hand through the rough spots and brilliantly helped me organize my thinking.

My two sons, Max and Chad, have given their mother peace in which to sew their whole lives. They've eaten many a Subway sandwich and frozen pizza for dinner over the years while their dad was out flying jets for a living, and I thank them for that, too. Esther, it's great quilting with you.

And Robert, beloved friend and husband, oblivious to my crazy quilting but *most* attentive to my happiness … I thank you most of all.

Preface

Crazy in the Garden, 46″ × 46″, by the author, 2009

The three-dimensional flowers took center stage here. I also added some machine embroidery of hummingbirds and beaded butterfly motifs to increase the richness of the mix. Details from this quilt are on pages 24, 50, and 53, as well as on the front cover.

This quilt won second place in the Embellished Quilts category at the 2010 International Quilt Festival in Houston, Texas.

Detail of *Bryant Family Cottage*, by the author, 2009

My first quilt was made of red and blue bandanas from the army surplus store, sewed together in a checkerboard. The batting was two heavy woolen blankets, and I used an old sheet for the backing. It was 1972, my brother was getting married, and the quilt weighed 25 pounds!

I've quilted ever since. My years as a design student in college have served me well in this passionate pursuit. Innumerable bed quilts, stained-glass quilts, and years of Broderie Perse and landscape quilts followed. I explored and loved them all for decades. But then crazy quilting happened to me in 2001, and my quilting life changed for good. I went from "sane" to "crazy," and I have never looked back.

People come to crazy quilting from many different disciplines: embroidery, painting, graphic arts, cross-stitching, and, nowadays, mixed media. All have found their way to this quilting genre, which embraces and accepts all needlework techniques, and they all bring their own special strengths to their stitching. But I come from a "sane," or traditional, quilting background, and it is *that* orientation that informs this book.

My goal is to make crazy quilting accessible to anyone who has been intrigued by the possibilities of this genre but intimidated by the technical challenges (and there are a few) or by the perception of the time required. Perhaps the overwhelming choices available in unfamiliar supplies have held people back from trying this incredibly satisfying and stimulating pastime. Or maybe, it is just plain hard to get started on something new.

I hope you will find what you need in this book to help you break through any reluctance and give crazy quilting a try. The first four chapters cover materials and techniques for creating your own "fabrics," constructing crazy blocks, and making wonderful embellishments using embroidery, ribbon, beads, and more. Then, there is a gallery of some of my fellow stitchers' work, as well as my own, to give you more ideas for your own work. Next you'll find six different and approachable projects that give you an opportunity to apply what you've learned. Some of these projects might take a weekend, while others will take longer; but all of them are designed to help you enter this fabulous world of stitching, texture, color, and, most of all, joy. Finally, the chapter titled Work in Progress: A Crazy Quilt from Start to Finish (pages 109–125) leads you through the entire process of creating a crazy quilt, with much information gleaned from hard experience.

I hope you enjoy it all and that you find this book useful. Joyful stitching, everybody!

—*Allie*

Collecting Your Materials and Tools

*P*eople come to crazy quilting from so many different backgrounds. Traditional makers of quilts go "crazy," of course, but many crazy quilters start out in embroidery, cross-stitching, painting, tatting, or even mixed media. And truly, any needlework or fiber technique can be incorporated into a crazy quilt. That's what keeps it so fresh with possibilities.

But some of these creative endeavors with crazy quilts involve slightly different supplies, materials, and tools than you may be used to working with. This is not to say that you need to go out and spend a lot of money to get started with crazy quilting. Much of what you'll need is closer at hand than you think. In fact, you might be one of those people who has hoarded and collected shiny and beautiful bits and mementos for years, wondering what to do with them. These bits are perfect for your crazy quilt! But if you aren't one of those people, this chapter will describe some sources for assembling the necessary goodies, as well as the kinds of tools you'll need.

Materials

We have more luscious choices than ever to include in our crazy quilts. We can even create our own "fabrics" to add to our quilts, using new supplies and techniques (page 19). Let's look at this sumptuous array of materials....

This detail of *Crazy in the Desert* (full quilt on page 65) shows a rich combination of burlap, commercially printed and hand-dyed cotton, upholstery, silks, and other fabrics, all looking like they very much belong together.

Fabrics

Traditionally, crazy quilts are made from "fancy" fabrics, such as silk and velvet, and indeed these fabrics are wonderful to use. But I love the great variety in texture, weave, fiber content, and even reflectivity that can be achieved by juxtaposing wildly divergent and unusual fabrics.

Ultrasuede, burlap, upholstery fabric, and corduroy look terrific in a block next to dupioni silk or commercially printed cotton. Wool and netted lace were made for each other. Shall we appliqué bonded lamé onto sueded rayon? Why not? And hand-dyed cotton looks great pieced in with brocade!

Left to right: Rayon panne velvet, silk brocade, Japanese cotton indigo, Ultrasuede, metallic knit, upholstery fabric, burlap

Left to right: Quilters' cotton, printed denim, rayon jacquard, woven Mylar, cotton velveteen, quilters' cotton, upholstery fabric

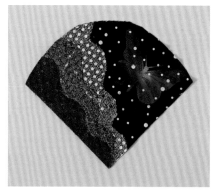

This is what crazy quilter Martha Green calls "pyrotechnics"—synthetic fabrics with Mylar "sequins" and holographic printing. Every fabric is fair game in crazy quilting.

But where can you find all these new-to-you fabrics? The number one source of choice for unusual and inexpensive textile finds is a thrift store. You may find a vintage silk blouse with a stain on the front for 50 cents, and it might even have nice buttons. Simply harvest the fabric (and buttons) by cutting the blouse apart and trimming off its construction sewing. In this way, you can add something unique (and inexpensive) to your stash.

Other finds include wedding gowns, prom dresses, and curtains, all of which give high yields of usable fabric. Jars of buttons that sell for a few dollars might very well contain some real treasures. So scout those thrift stores, yard and estate sales, flea markets, and swap meets, too.

Cut-up old clothes become great fabrics!

Sometimes old linens, such as hankies or tea towels, make a great base for embroidery and crazy quilting. You can even include traditional vintage quilt blocks in your crazy quilts.

Collect linens, hankies, and blocks. For crazy quilt projects that "upcycle" these finds, see *Waltie* (page 81) and *"Sisters" Crazy Quilt Scrapbook Page* (page 88).

Upholstery shops are another great place to find an array of unique fabrics. Most have outdated sample books just waiting for the trash. Offer to take these off their hands and get a whole palette of 4″ × 6″ fabrics in just one book. You don't need much of any one fabric at all for a crazy quilt. The more variety you include, the better (in my opinion). You'll be saving the landfill, too.

Upholstery samples

Always check out the remnant bins at high-end fabric shops. Likewise, some silk import companies, such as Thai Silks in Los Altos, California (see Suppliers, page 127), may sometimes sell beautiful packs of outdated samples for a few dollars apiece.

Another great way to enhance your fabric stash is via online swaps. Many crazy quilt groups facilitate well-organized exchanges of fabrics—usually around a theme—among their members. Poke around on the Internet to see what you can find. Groups are full of friendly people who would love to share their passion for CQ (crazy quilting) with you and help you get involved, and the groups are easy to join.

Quilt shops and chain fabric stores will always provide tempting additions to your stash. You only need to buy ⅛ yard of any one fabric as you are getting started.

One last mysterious, but true, thought about acquiring fabrics: When word gets out that you have taken up crazy quilting, all kinds of strange and wonderful textiles will come to you from people who don't know what to do with them but who want to see them used. You will become a fabric magnet. When a friend of mine sold her family's custom jet upholstery business, a station wagon full of *very* interesting sample books and swatches came my way. (There must be some amazing private jets out there. My imagination's favorite private jet is done up in pink faux leopard tapestry fabric!)

Threads

I was a "sane" quilter for a long time. The only threads I ever used were for machine piecing, quilting, and appliqué. So when crazy quilting took over my life, I had to start building my thread stash from scratch. Dull or shiny, thick or thin, smooth or hairy—threads give you so many design options.

I remember when all the embroidery thread I owned fit in one little box! Now my thread fills many, many small bins. Needlepoint and cross-stitch stores and websites, exchanges with friends, online purveyors catering especially to the crazy quilter, eBay and Etsy shops—all are great places to look for new and interesting threads.

Let's examine some different kinds of threads and see how they look stitched up. This is not a comprehensive list—just threads I like and use a lot.

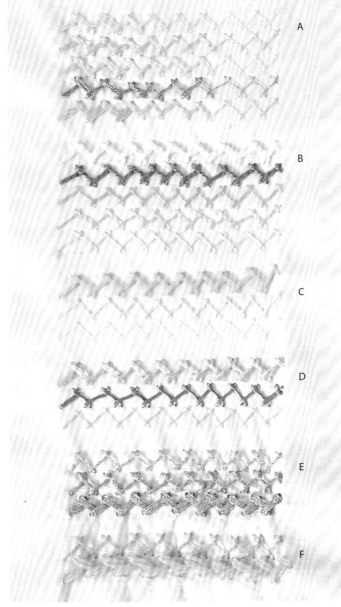

Thread sampler

On this thread sampler, the threads are all used in the herringbone stitch for comparison purposes.

A Embroidery floss, made of separate strands. *Top to bottom:* Bamboo, rayon, cotton, metallic, and silk, each shown stitched in 6 strands, 3 strands, and 1 strand. These are the most common and versatile threads used in crazy quilting.

B Perle threads, with twisted strands. *Top to bottom:* Cotton, size 3 and 5; rayon and silk, size 8; and fine silk, size 12. The higher the number, the thinner the thread. The twist in perle thread gives luster to your stitches.

C Single-strand threads. *Top to bottom:* Nylon "velvet" thread, DMC cotton flower thread, and Guttermann machine silk thread. Single-strand thread, whether thick or thin, gives stitches a clean line.

D Non-plied threads. *Top to bottom:* Rayon, silk from Kreinik, and Scalamandré fine silk. These threads are slightly more difficult to work with, because you have to make sure they stay twisted as you stitch. But you can't get their sheen any other way.

E Kreinik metallics. *Top to bottom:* Fine braid, medium braid, and ⅛" metallic ribbon. Kreinik (see Suppliers, page 127) is the go-to company for glittery threads, in my opinion. Its threads are easy to work with and come in so many fine colors, weights, and types.

F Wool. *Top to bottom:* Medicis fine tapestry yarn by DMC and 3-ply needlepoint yarn. Wool is always a pleasure to stitch with, and it lends a folksy look to your needlework. It also contrasts so nicely with silk.

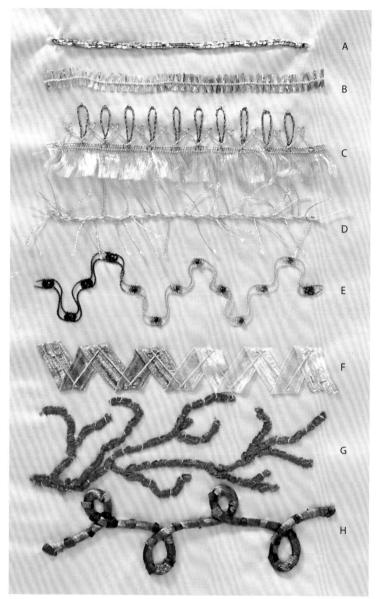

Sampler of unusual threads

A Mylar-wrapped rayon by Mokuba (see Suppliers, page 127)

B Metallic eyelash

C Feathery eyelash attached with Kreinik metallic embroidery thread in herringbone and detached chain stitch

D Rayon eyelash

E Eyelash couched with seed beads

F Rayon ribbon couched with her-ringbone stitch in DMC Flower thread

G Chenille yarn couched with machine quilting thread

H Rayon cording couched with hand-dyed 4mm silk ribbon

You can use interesting selections from your local knitting shop. These fibers generally need to be couched down (attached to the quilt surface with hand stitches, using a second thread) rather than stitched with directly.

Trims

Trims are such an easy way to add complexity to the look of crazy quilting. Whether sewn on by themselves, grouped (see *Crazy Quilt Soft Doll: The Dreaming Maiden*, page 101), or used as the base for further hand embellishment, trims are an indispensable element in crazy quilting.

A Metallic and cotton woven braid

B Wide chenille rickrack

C Rayon rickrack with woven detail

D Machine-embroidered cotton rickrack

E Rayon jacquard from Ally's Bazaar (see Suppliers, page 127)

F Narrow rayon guimp

G Circle-stitched rayon guimp

H Solid rayon guimp

I Rayon cording

J French jacquard–woven rayon trim

Trim sampler

You only need to buy half a yard at a time. However, if you *really* like one trim in particular, then 2 or 3 yards will last you for a while. I buy my trims at sewing and specialty stores, from vendors at quilt shows, or anywhere I can find them!

Lace

Lace adds elegance and charm to crazy quilts. There are so many kinds of lace, and they are all so pretty. You'll find vintage lace at estate sales, thrift stores, and antique shops, to name a few places. When word gets out that you are a crazy quilter, prepare to become a lace magnet. Many people save it, but they don't know how to use it. So they'll give it to you for your crazy quilts … and you'll be doing them a favor by taking it off their hands!

Fabric stores catering to the bridal sewer are your best bet for purchasing new lace. And as with trim, you don't need very much of any one kind.

There is so much the crazy quilter can do with lace, including beading it, embroidering over it, and painting it (pages 41–43).

Lace sampler. Note especially the crocheted lace, third from the bottom, which has rickrack attached!

Silk ribbon

Silk ribbon embroidery is another area of interest to the crazy quilter. You can use 2, 4, 7, 13mm, or wider widths either in the embroidery along and over the seams, between your fabric patches or shapes (from here on called *seam treatments*), or in designs within the shapes, called *motifs*.

Silk ribbon in various widths and special long-eyed needles (page 15) used to stitch with them

❧ Tools

Crazy quilting is low-tech, and you don't need to invest much money to practice it. This is, of course, because most of the work is done by hand. If you do use a sewing machine to create blocks, a very simple machine will suffice. Almost the only machine stitches I ever use are the straight stitch and the zigzag. (*The Beach at Pilar, San Carlos, Mexico*, on page 93, does offer a chance to use some of your machine's embroidery stitches, however.)

Sharp embroidery, fabric, and paper scissors; an iron and ironing surface; a rotary cutter, ruler, and mat; good lighting; a simple design wall surface (page 18)—these are the only basics you need. If you prefer to embroider using a hoop, that is another essential but inexpensive tool; some crazy quilters swear by them, while others (myself included) can't stand them. One special thing you *will* need, though, is lots of different kinds and sizes of needles.

Basic sewing supplies, with an emphasis on different kinds of needles, are all you need for crazy quilting.

Needles

Different-sized threads require larger and smaller needles, so start collecting them. Needles are not expensive, so buy them in an array of sizes. You will never have enough needles! Here is a good selection to start with.

- Large-eyed chenilles or crewel embroidery needles, used for ribbon embroidery

- Milliner's (or straw) needles, good for French knots because the eye isn't wider than the shaft

- Embroidery needles, for all-around work

- Beading needles—15s for very small beads and 11s for normal seed beads, crystals, and such

A large pincushion to keep track of all these needles is important, too. The first project shows how to make one (page 70).

Special tools

Large-eyed needles sometimes require a small pair of pliers to pull them through the fabric, especially if they are threaded with heavy yarn or a narrow piece of lace or trim.

In the photo (above right), the pliers have been used to pull the cording to the back of the block. Note that the shorter the tail of cording hanging out the eye of the needle, the easier it will be to pull through to the back of the block. A ¼"–½" tail is sufficient.

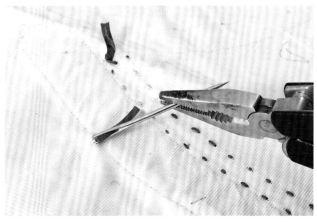

Use pliers to pull cording through.

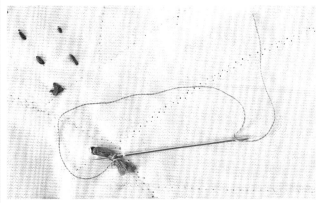

Secure the end of the cording to the back with a few stitches of thread.

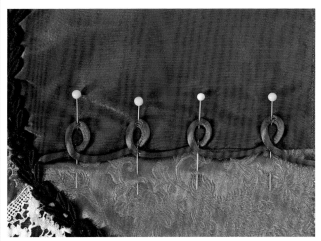

This cording comes neatly through from the back and is pinned in place, ready to sew down.

Another special tool is the Creative Textile Tool by Walnut Hollow (see Suppliers, page 127). This optional, but very handy, tool is like an electric wood-burning tool but is specifically made for fibers. With it you can cut out and seal synthetic fabrics to make petals and so forth, as well as seal the ends of rayon ribbon to prevent them from raveling. It can also be used as a burnisher to transfer certain printed images onto fabric (page 22).

Tip

It's really helpful to have a designated place to work—even if it is just a large tray—where you can leave out your project, supplies, and tools, without having to gather them up after each work session.

Marking tools and tricks

For many, marking tools and templates are also necessary for crazy quilting. These tools will help ensure that your stitching is even in your seam treatments. They are also helpful guidelines for embroidered motifs within shapes.

For light-colored fabrics, I use a disappearing-ink pen or light pencil mark. For darker fabrics, a white chalk pencil works well. However, if you need a fine line, a light-colored gel pen is great. *Important:* A gel pen mark is permanent, so make sure to cover the line with embellishments. Experiment to find out what works best for you.

Some templates are specifically designed for crazy quilters to help with seam treatments in preparation for many kinds of stitches. Let's have a look at these special templates.

DREAM-A-SEAM

Carole Samples, one of the all-time great crazy quilters of our era, has designed an extensive set of plastic Dream-A-Seam templates, which can be purchased online from a variety of sources (see Suppliers, page 127). Dream-A-Seam templates are great for round shapes, which are so hard to get right when drawn freehand. You can also combine the templates to get a more complex seam treatment.

With Dream-A-Seam templates, simply place the template over the seam and mark around it.

SUCCESS STRIPS

Success Strips, by Creative Stitchery (see Suppliers, page 127), are see-through rulers with holes placed at different intervals and heights. With these rulers, just mark the dots on your block, depending on which stitch you will use and what size you wish to make it. Then simply follow the dots. You could also use your carefully marked and stitched seam as the base for more additions that won't require marking.

With Success Strips, accurate stitching is simple—just follow the dots. (You can also use the pattern in the guimp trim itself to space beads or stitches.)

This postcard by Jo Newsham of New Zealand shows the fabulous results you can get from using the Success Strips.

MAKE A PAPER TEMPLATE

You can also make your own paper templates to serve as marking guides for stitching. To do this, cut a strip of paper to the length and shape of your seam, accordion fold it (like a paper doll chain), mark one edge with your pattern, cut it, and unfold it.

Homemade templates can be particularly helpful on curved seams. Place tracing paper over the curved seam you wish to embellish and draw a line over the seam to get the exact curve. Then decide how wide you want your seam embellishment stitching to be and on which side of the seam your stitching will be. Draw a line to that width, parallel to the first drawn line. Then fold the strip like a paper doll chain, with each section the same length. Draw the desired shape along the outer edge of the paper and cut it out through all the folds. This technique could be used for a scallop shape or perhaps small triangles, as shown at right. Unfold and pin the paper template onto your block, lining up the first drawn line with the seamline. Then trace along the shaped outer edge onto the fabric.

It might take a few tries to get the template you want, but remember—it's only tracing paper!

Left to right: Draw a curved paper template, fold, cut, and pin in place.

Note

An alternative to placing embroidery next to a seam is to straddle the seam on both sides with embroidery stitching. In this case, be sure to allow for a little extra paper on one side so that your folded paper template does not fall apart.

USE WASTE CANVAS

Waste canvas is a grid held together by water-soluble glue. It is most often used by cross-stitchers and is available at craft and needlework shops in different-sized grids. You can baste a strip of the grid along a seam on your block, decide on a pattern to stitch, and then use the grid as a guide—as in counted cross-stitch—to produce very precise stitching.

After all the embroidery is completed through the holes in the mesh, remove the grid fibers one by one with tweezers. Some stitchers like to dampen the waste canvas first to loosen the glue, but I've never found that to be necessary.

Four different shapes have been stitched; grids are in various stages of removal.

I would like to thank cross-stitch designer Pamela Kellogg for explaining how to apply the waste canvas concept to crazy quilt stitching in such an innovative way. (See *"Sisters" Crazy Quilt Scrapbook Page*, Steps 5–7, on page 91, for another great use of waste canvas.)

OTHER SIMPLE TECHNIQUES

Plastic mesh circles, which are used for plastic canvas stitching, can be found in craft stores and literally cost just pennies. They are excellent for marking different sizes of circles, especially when making flowers (pages 43 and 44).

Your sewing machine sews evenly, doesn't it? You can use the basting stitch and the zigzag to mark even spacing for your stitching. When you are done, just pull out the machine stitching.

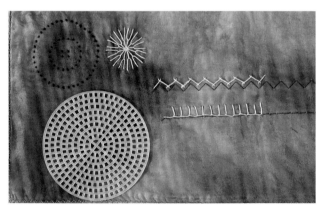

Left: The plastic mesh circle was used to mark; the motif in white was stitched using these marks. *Right:* Lines of sewing machine stitching (in red) were used as a guide for hand stitching.

One last word: You can always eyeball your work and stitch with no marking at all. To be honest, that is what I do 90 percent of the time!

How to make a design wall

The final tool that any crazy quilter can benefit from is the design wall. I think it is so important to be able to view your work in progress on a vertical surface.

My design wall consists of a large piece of batting tacked up on a blank wall—nothing fancy.

If wall space is an issue, the easiest way to get that design wall surface is to hang a piece of batting cut to fit over a door. Judie Bellingham of www.bellaonline.com has a great design for this that she has agreed to share.

WHAT YOU'LL NEED

- Cotton batting
- 2 lengths of dowel, 1¼″ diameter, cut the width of your door
- Sewing machine
- Thread

1. Use a tape measure to measure from the very top of your door to 6″ below the handle. Add 12″ to that length. Cut the batting to this length × the width of the door.

2. To make rod pockets for the dowels, turn over the top and bottom ends of the batting by 6″ and sew them using a straight stitch.

3. Slip the dowels into the pockets and hang one end over the door.

Whichever option you choose, it is important to have a place where you can look at your work as it evolves.

Creating Your Own "Fabrics"

The Russian Lace, 15" × 15", by the author, 2009

So many new techniques for working with fibers, fabrics, and imagery are available in the textile world. Many of these techniques can be integrated into crazy quilting. They really give crazy quilts an updated, contemporary look and feel, taking crazy quilting out of the traditional Victorian mold for good! Of course, if you love the Victorians, as many do in the crazy quilting world, these innovations in textile work can help there, too.

Transferring your own imagery onto fabric, adding your own designs with stencils, "making" your own fabric with Angelina fibers—all of these techniques have brought a new age to crazy quilting. I am sure you have many more techniques to add, but my favorites here seem especially suited to crazy quilting.

Detail of *Crazy for Flowers* (full quilt on page 66)

❧ Image Transfer

In *Crazy for Flowers* (full quilt on page 66), the three-dimensional embellished flowers on the left of the block are mimicked on the right side by pink plum blossoms, which were photographed, printed on fabric, and pieced into the block.

Transferring your chosen imagery onto fabric is such an exciting way to add a personal element to your work. Although there are many great books on the subject (including *Secrets of Digital Quilting—From Camera to Quilt*, by Lura Schwarz Smith and Kerby C. Smith, from C&T Publishing), I will present here my own streamlined techniques, devised after many years of experimenting (and countless bad prints, I might add). Please remember to *always* test your print on paper before committing to using it on your precious fabric.

Home inkjet printer

For sharp, wonderful imagery, I recommend the commercially prepared-for-printing EQ Printables cotton fabric sheets, made by the Electric Quilt Company (see Suppliers, page 127). These sheets are the best I've found for this purpose. However, if you want to prepare your own fabric for printing, follow the directions in this section.

Inkjet printers use two different kinds of inks, pigment based and dye based, depending on the manufacturer. The pigment inks rest on the fabric's surface, while the dye molecules bond with the fiber molecules of the fabric. Dye-based inks require the fabric to be pretreated to accept the dye, while pigment-based inks do not. I always pretreat my fabrics for my pigment ink printer anyway, because doing so gives me a sharper print. Bubble Jet Set is the best-known pretreatment product.

You can get a great print from either ink, if you know a few basic tricks. But be aware that pigment-based inks are believed to be more lightfast than dye-based inks.

PREPARING YOUR FABRIC

1. Always prewash fabric to get any manufacturer's finishing chemicals (or sizing) out of it. These chemicals can interfere with the dye or pigment and prevent it from bonding or adhering to the fabric.

2. Soak the fabric briefly in Bubble Jet Set, following the manufacturer's directions. Then gently wring it out and air dry.

3. Iron the fabric. To enable it to go through the printer, it needs a carrier to make it stiff enough. Many people use freezer paper for this. However, I have found that the most foolproof carrier is full-sheet 8½" × 11" label paper. The fabric sticks to it very evenly and will not jam in your printer. Iron the fabric once it is adhered to the label paper and make sure there are no bubbles or wrinkles.

4. Trim the fabric to exactly the size of your paper, using a rotary cutter, mat, and see-through ruler. Make sure no threads are hanging off the edges.

5. To make it easier to remove after printing, clip off a tiny corner of the label paper before you smooth and then iron it onto your pretreated fabric.

Tip

Keep a lint roller handy to pick up any flecks of fiber or thread from both sides of your fabric before you adhere it to the label paper. Do this again before you run the fabric through your printer. Otherwise, these threads will act as tiny stencils—when you pull them off your print, they will leave little white lines where the ink couldn't get to the fabric.

6. Print on the fabric. Let it dry at least an hour (it should be longer, but who can wait?). Iron it lightly on the back to soften the label paper adhesive, pull off the label, and rinse the print in water or Bubble Jet Set Rinse, if you have some. Do not wring. Instead, allow the fabric to air dry and then iron it. You are now ready to incorporate your image into your crazy quilt.

June, 15½″ × 11¼″, by the author, 2010. Transfer Artist Paper (TAP) sheets are featured.

Iron-on inkjet transfer sheets

These sheets, which can be purchased at any craft or quilting store, are commonly known as T-shirt transfer sheets. With these sheets, you choose a digital image that you wish to print. You must mirror image, or horizontal flip, your image first, because you will be placing the image face-down on fabric when you iron it on. If you don't reverse it, everything will look backward.

Read and carefully follow the manufacturer's instructions. I like to use a tightly woven cotton and smaller motifs. An iron set to "no steam" and a flat surface are all you need.

These sheets offer a reliable method for getting a great image. The drawback is that the surface of the image ends up with a "plasticky" feel. In addition, stitching through it takes a little extra work, and the needle will leave permanent holes. However, for an accent image, this is a cheap and easy way to go.

For a crisp, detailed look, Transfer Artist Paper (TAP) is a quality transfer sheet that changes the hand of the fabric less than some of the other brands (see Suppliers, page 127).

Sheet of transfer paper with several Victorian images, with one image transferred onto cotton fabric

Details of *The Russian Lace* (full quilt on page 19), showing a laser-transferred image in the center and inkjet-printed fabrics used in piecing and appliquéd as motifs

Laser print transfer

Another way to transfer printed images from paper requires the use of a laser printer. If you have access to a home laser printer, it will give you a better print to sew with than the transfer paper, because the hand of the fabric is not affected.

Two good fabric choices for this technique are tightly woven cotton or polyester bridal satin. You will need your reversed digital images printed on normal paper with a home laser printer (*not* a commercial laser copy machine), a heated burnishing tool to transfer the toner from the paper to the fabric, and a flat, heatproof surface. Wood Hollow's Creative Textile Tool (see Suppliers, page 127) and the tempered glass surface sold with it work very well. You can also use a small piece of Masonite or heavy illustration board as a burnishing surface.

Be advised that it takes a little practice to get a perfect print and that smaller images are easier to work with than larger ones. (The printed images are great as motifs.) Different copiers or printers may give you varied results on different kinds of fabrics. Be sure to experiment on scraps of fabric to get a feel for this process. Take some time to play.

And please, don't burn your fingers. Be careful!

1. Have your selected image reverse printed by a laser printer.

2. Tape the fabric right side up on a smooth hard surface so that it doesn't slip. The surface must be able to withstand heat.

3. Place the laser print facedown on the fabric.

4. Make sure your burnishing tool has had plenty of time to warm up before you start. Press the tool hard all over the surface of the back of the paper. Don't leave the tool in one spot for too long, or it will cause the paper to stick to the fabric. Use the edge of the tool, pressing hard in a back-and-forth motion, as if you were coloring hard with a crayon. You want the toner to melt and transfer to the fabric, and that takes pressure.

5. Lift a corner of the paper to see if you need to keep applying the heat and pressure. If your print looks good, peel off the paper. There is your print!

Laser prints, on paper and transferred onto fabric: The two prints on the bottom left are on poly bridal satin; the two on the bottom right are on a tight-weave cotton. *Images from the collection of Patricia Winter*

Crazy quilt tote bag with stenciled fabric, made by the author, 2008

✤ Stenciling

I also use stencils to create designs on fabric or to create motifs, such as the central flower image in the tote bag (above). These stencils often become the focal point for a crazy quilt project. There are many ways to use stencils; the one I like involves painting thickened craft ink through the stenciled design.

Tsukineko inks are very versatile for putting color on fiber. A great trick for using them in stenciling (or any fabric painting) is to thicken them with clear aloe gel—any brand from the drugstore will do, as long as it is clear. Simply mix a little of the ink with a small squirt of aloe on the plate. Use a fine brush, adding a little color at a time to paint the thickened ink into the spaces created by the stencil.

After the fabric has had plenty of time to dry, remove the stencil and heat set the ink with your iron; then rinse and dry the fabric. I used my stencil as the focal point of a tote bag, adding some fine stipple machine quilting around the image before piecing it into my tote front.

Detail of the stenciled fabric pieced into a crazy quilt tote bag

This stencil by the Stewart Gill Company was painted using aloe-thickened Tsukineko ink.

Detail of *Crazy in the Garden* (full quilt on page 5). This embroidered Angelina butterfly was created by Catherine Smith of Newberg, Oregon. She gave me five butterflies for this quilt.

❦ Angelina

Angelina, a glittery, fun accent, is easy to work with to create "fabric" for crazy quilts. Because the fused sheet of fibers is nonwoven, you can cut out shapes from Angelina with no fraying of the edges. You can then sew through it or machine embroider onto it. I love using Angelina to make three-dimensional flower petals. (See the lilac flower on page 51.) When making "fabric," I often fuse my Angelina sheet with fusible web to a fabric backing—this makes it sturdier for the handling that comes with embellishing a block.

1. Arrange bondable Angelina fibers between 2 sheets of waxed paper. You can mix different colors of fibers if you choose. (*Note:* Not all Angelina fibers are bondable.)

2. With an iron set on silk, iron the waxed paper and Angelina "sandwich" for a just few seconds to melt the fibers to each other, forming a sheet. The more fibers you use, the thicker the sheet will be.

3. Lift a corner of the top sheet of waxed paper to make sure the fibers have bonded. If they haven't, iron again briefly or turn up the iron's temperature. Turn over the waxed paper sandwich and iron from the back for a few seconds as well.

Tip

The longer you heat the Angelina, the duller the fibers become. Therefore it is recommended that you iron them only as long as it takes to melt them.

Left to right: Angelina laid out on paper; Angelina fused into a sheet; the sheet fused onto silk habotai

Machine embroiderers can create lovely motifs on Angelina, which can then be cut out and appliquéd to a crazy quilt.

Add some sparkle and texture! Fuse a thin sheet of Angelina to a piece of fabric and then piece it into a block.

Angelina fused to cotton/silk blend and then pieced into a block

My favorite use for Angelina is for making flower petals.

These petals were made from sheets of Angelina that were fused with Lite Steam-A-Seam 2 onto silk. They were then cut out and sewn to the base fabric with beads.

Tip

All this fusing can get a little messy on your ironing board. A simple preventive solution is to cut off a piece of freezer paper and iron it directly onto the ironing board cover where you will be working. When you've finished fusing all your Angelina and fabric sandwiches, peel off the freezer paper and toss.

Detail of *A Work in Progress* by author

Four Ways to Build a Crazy Quilt Block

Granddaughter's Flower Garden, 19½″ × 19½″, by the author, 2008

In this quilt, the center elements, including some vintage Grandma's Flower Garden blocks on the four sides, were machine appliquéd and hand embroidered. The herringbone embroidery along the "seams" in the border highlights the edges of the fabric pieces.

How you construct your crazy quilt blocks depends on the way you prefer to work and the look you are trying to achieve. Though they use differing techniques, all the methods presented here require the use of a foundation fabric, most commonly muslin. To attach fabrics to muslin, you can use one of four methods:

- Piece them on with your sewing machine, using the foundation piecing method (sometimes known as "sew and flip").

- Appliqué them by hand or machine.

- Fuse them.

- Randomly chain piece them on your machine and sew the chunks onto your foundation.

Some of these methods allow you to exactly replicate a block diagram that you wish to use. Others give you a free-form approach, in which the finished block will be inspired by the original block design but will become an ongoing sewing adventure that doesn't reveal itself until you are done. The "chunk" method, in particular, has much of this randomness built into it, as you will see.

I often enjoy not knowing where I am headed when I commence constructing blocks. This technique can create that random look that so many vintage crazy quilts have. Other times, however, I need complete control of my design from the beginning, so I know that what I have planned is what I will achieve when I am done sewing. And then, of course, there is that middle ground— preplanning is involved, but there is room for serendipitous design decision making along the way, too.

Let's look at these four methods in detail, so you can figure out what will work best for you.

❧ METHOD 1
foundation piecing

Let's start with the most common construction method for crazy quilt blocks, foundation piecing. Here, we'll practice foundation piecing, first using shapes with straight edges and then using those with gently curved edges.

Straight-edge foundation piecing

In this exercise, we'll piece an 8" × 8" block with 9 shapes.

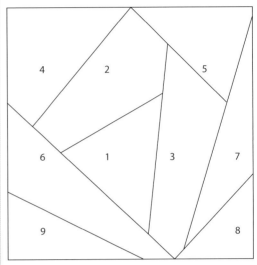

Block diagram

WHAT YOU'LL NEED

- 10" × 10" piece of muslin for the foundation

- 8" × 8" pieces of 9 fancy fabrics

- 10" × 10" piece of lightweight fusible knit interfacing (*optional*, but recommended)

- Water-soluble marker

- Tracing paper and pencil

- Scissors that you don't mind using on fabric *and* tracing paper

IMPORTANT: The lines on the foundation block are drawn to aid in placing the shapes; they are not sewing lines. These lines help you eyeball your shape placement.

1. Using the block diagram (page 27) as a reference, draw an 8″ × 8″ block with 9 straight-edge shapes on a piece of paper.

2. Place the muslin over the diagram and trace the lines with the water-soluble marker onto the muslin. Use a lightbox or window for this step.

3. Trace the first shape onto tracing paper, adding a ½″ seam allowance all the way around. Mark the shape number. Cut out the pattern piece, including the seam allowance.

4. Pin the shape 1 pattern onto the fabric, right sides up, and cut it out, remembering to retain those seam allowances.

5. Lay shape 1 directly onto its marked place on the muslin block, right side up. Stitch around its perimeter to hold it in place.

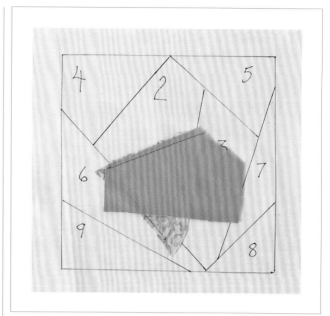

Shape 2 sewn on shape 1

8. Flip up shape 2 and iron it flat. (*Note:* Iron after every patch is sewn and flipped.)

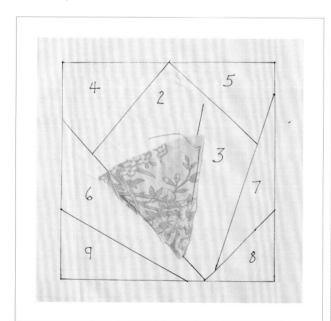

Shape 1 sewn into place

6. Repeat Steps 3 and 4 for shape 2.

7. Pin shape 2 in place, right sides together with shape 1. Be sure that once sewn and flipped, the shape completely covers the area you want. Sew the seam as shown.

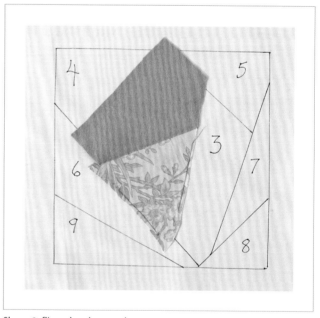

Shape 2, flipped and pressed

9. Repeat Steps 3 and 4 and Steps 7 and 8 for shape 3. If necessary, add a little stay stitching to the very outside edges of each shape after you add them to the muslin foundation.

10. Repeat Steps 3 and 4 and Steps 7 and 8 for shapes 4–9 to complete piecing the block. These shapes all include perimeter edges of the block. For these outside edges, when cutting out the fabric pieces, add a 1″ seam allowance for ease of trimming later. As in Step 9, if necessary, add stay stitching to the very outside edges of each shape after adding them to the muslin foundation.

11. On your completed pieced block, draw a stitching line exactly 8″ × 8″ square to show the finished block size. This will guide you so you will know how far to extend the hand embroidery, or seam treatment, along the seams. Stitch on the drawn line.

12. Zigzag stitch around the perimeter of the block. With all the handling your blocks will receive as you embellish them, those edges will otherwise fray.

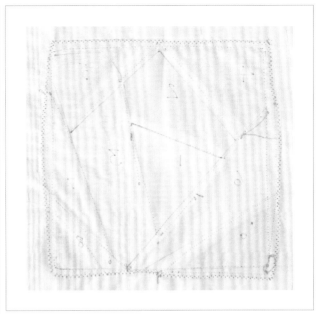

Back of finished block

Completed pieced block

Optional: After giving your block one last pressing, fuse some knit interfacing onto the back. This stabilizes the block. For me, it also obviates the need for an embroidery hoop while I am embellishing.

After embellishing the block, trim it to 8½″ × 8½″, which includes ¼″ seam allowances (or, if you prefer, trim to 9″ × 9″ for ½″ seam allowances). Then zigzag stitch around its perimeter before assembling it into a quilt as an 8″ × 8″ finished block.

Tip

If you are going to add beads later, do not bead right up to the 8″ finished edge. Instead, give yourself a ¼″ margin inside the finished block boundaries for any beadwork. Have you ever broken a sewing machine needle sewing over a bead? It is a jarring experience!

Tips

Here are a few piecing tips.

- Interface any fancy fabrics that ravel or wiggle, such as charmeuse silk or velvet, so that they are easier to piece. Lay out small scraps of the fabric that you will be using upside down on an ironing surface. (Place velvet on terrycloth, so as not to crush the nap when you iron it.) Place the interfacing over the fabric, making sure that the glue side is against the fabric; then, fuse.

- Protect your iron when fusing by placing a piece of tracing paper between the iron and the fusible interfacing. Wonder Under release paper (the paper on the back) works well for this, too.

- After you've fused, turn over the fabrics. If there are any bubbles caused by the interfacing, just press them out. For velvet, press out any bubbles from the back to avoid crushing the nap.

- When piecing on a shape of heavier fabric, such as the brocade upholstery fabric used in shape 3 (photo at right), flip the block over after sewing it on. Then press this seam flat from the back first to keep the foundation muslin from distorting.

- Before flipping and pressing a shape into place, carefully trim back any seam allowance that is too bulky. Sometimes you might even reduce bulk by "grading" your seam allowances (trimming the top one to a smaller width than the one beneath it) or by clipping and notching the curves.

- Don't sew over the pins; instead, remove them as you go along.

Curved-edge foundation piecing

In this exercise, we'll make an 8″ × 8″ block with 9 shapes. This is the same block design as in Straight-Edge Foundation Piecing (pages 27–29), but the lines have been gently curved. Just about any block can be adapted to curved piecing in this way.

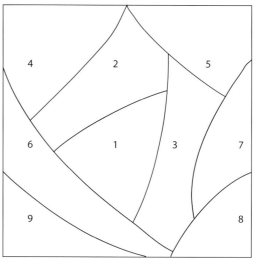

Block diagram

The material requirements and the piecing process are the same as in straight-edge foundation piecing, except that the shapes are pinned into place before sewing them to the foundation. See Tips (at left) for additional information.

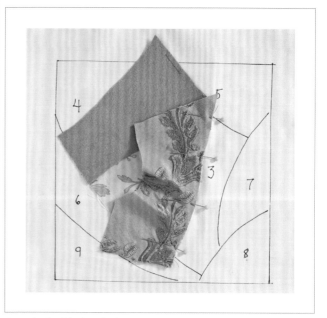

Curved-edge block with shape 3 pinned into place and ready for sewing

Completed curved-edge block

How to design your own blocks

It's not hard to design your own block diagrams! The best way is to make small sketches of a design you want to try; then refine it with overlays of tracing paper.

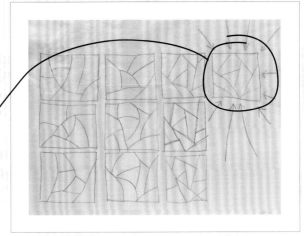

Sketches on tracing paper showing the evolution of the design used in method 1

My finished block design

As you sketch, think about the sequence, or order, in which you will be sewing the shapes onto foundation fabric. When you arrive at a block design that you are happy with, use a fresh piece of tracing paper and go over your design with a ruler and marker, so you will have a good, clean copy of your design with lines that show up well. Enlarge this design, either on a copier or by redrawing it and eyeballing the lines to correspond with your small design. Then decide on the piecing sequence and number the individual shapes in the order in which they will be sewn to the foundation fabric.

Next place a piece of muslin over your diagram, tape everything flat, and trace the diagram onto the muslin, using a light pencil or water-soluble pen. These lines will help you place your fabric shapes, no matter what construction method you choose for building your block.

❀ METHOD 2
freezer paper appliqué

If you prefer a different method for piecing curved seams than previously described (see Curved-Edge Foundation Piecing, page 30), or if you want a block that has more pronounced curves in its shapes, curved appliqué is the method to use. It allows you to be accurate and to work quite quickly. The secret is to use freezer paper templates.

WHAT YOU'LL NEED

- 10″ × 10″ piece of muslin for the foundation
- Small pieces of 10 fancy fabrics
- 10″ × 10″ piece of lightweight fusible knit interfacing (*optional*)
- 10″ × 10″ piece of freezer paper
- Clear monofilament thread
- Water-soluble marker
- Paper scissors

1. Using a lightbox or window, place the muslin over the block diagram and trace the lines with the water-soluble marker to aid with the placement of the shapes.

2. Using a lightbox or window, trace the finished block design onto freezer paper. Extend the lines of the shapes 1″ beyond the perimeter of the finished block, drawing to the edges of the paper (next column).

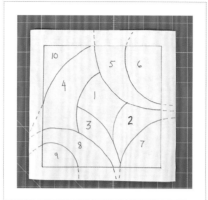

Block diagram traced onto freezer paper with an extra 1″ included at the perimeter edges of each shape.

3. Using paper-designated scissors, cut out the freezer paper shapes *plus the extra margins.*

Freezer paper shapes cut out. Note that the extra 1″ margin around the perimeter of the finished block is retained. This is important!

4. Decide which fabrics to use for each shape.

5. Iron the freezer paper templates onto the right side of the selected fabrics and cut them out, leaving a ½″ margin around all sides (except at the perimeter edges of the block, where a full 1″ margin is already included). Mark lightly around the freezer paper with a water-soluble marker (or any marker that will show up). These lines will help guide placement of the shapes as they are appliquéd to the block.

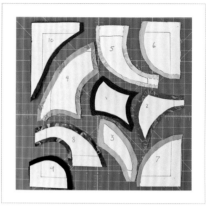

Freezer paper templates have been ironed on and fabrics cut out with seam allowances.

6. Place shape 1 on the foundation muslin and sew it in place around its perimeter.

7. Shape 2 will overlap the seam allowance of shape 1. Turn under the overlapping edge of shape 2, using the freezer paper template as a guide and clipping curves as necessary; press. The turned-under edge should correspond exactly to the cut-out freezer paper's edge. Remove the freezer paper.

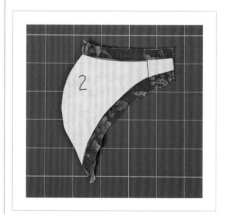

Shape 2 with ironed-under edge (left edge)

8. Pin shape 2 in place, overlapping shape 1. Appliqué with clear monofilament thread in a narrow zigzag stitch. (This could also be appliquéd by hand.)

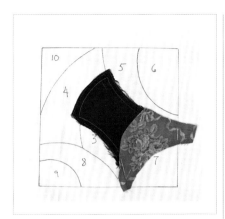

Shape 2 appliquéd into place over shape 1

9. Repeat Steps 7 and 8 with shapes 3–10.

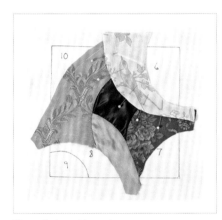

Shape 5 pinned into place
and ready to appliqué

10. Iron the block flat and machine zigzag stitch around the perimeter of the fancy fabrics. Then, and only then, mark and stitch the finished 8″ × 8″ size on the block.

Optional: Interface the back of the block with fusible knit interfacing.

After embellishing the block, trim it to 8½″ × 8½″, which includes ¼″ seam allowances (or, if you prefer, to 9″ × 9″ for ½″ seam allowances). Then zigzag stitch around its perimeter before assembling it into a quilt as an 8″ × 8″ finished block.

Completed block

❊ METHOD 3
fused appliqué

I particularly like fused appliqué when I know I will be using trim between the fabric shapes on my block. Although the fusible web causes some stiffness, I won't be hand embellishing through it, so the stiffness doesn't matter.

However, I don't fuse each entire shape to the background fabric; rather, I only fuse their edges, using Lite Steam-A-Seam 2 in the ¼″ and ½″ widths. This Steam-A-Seam product from the Warm Company comes on a roll, like tape, with a paper backing. To use it, simply tear off a piece the length needed for each edge of the patch and iron the pieces in place on the patches. Then peel off the paper, position each patch in the same sequence laid out in your block diagram, and fuse the patches into place, one by one.

In this example, I use the same 8″ × 8″ block diagram as in Curved-Edge Foundation Piecing (page 30) and a variation of the technique presented in Method 2: Freezer Paper Appliqué (page 32).

WHAT YOU'LL NEED

- 10″ × 10″ piece of muslin for the foundation

- Small pieces of 9 fancy fabrics

- 12″-long pieces of 8 different ½″-wide (minimum) decorative trims (page 13)

- ¼″- or ½″-wide Lite Steam-A-Seam 2

- 10″ × 10″ piece of freezer paper

- 10″ × 10″ piece of knit fusible interfacing (*optional*)

- Water-soluble marker

- Paper scissors

1. Follow Steps 1–5 of Method 2: Freezer Paper Appliqué (page 32), except for this important difference: Cut out a ¼″ *seam allowance* around each shape, leaving the 1″ seam allowance around all perimeter edges, as before.

2. On the back of each cut-out shape, follow the manufacturer's directions to fuse a strip of ¼″ Lite Steam-A-Seam 2 along each edge. Leave the backing paper in place. I prefer to use the ¼″ Lite Steam-A-Seam 2 tape with this method instead of the ½″, because it creates less stiffness in the block and less bulk in the narrower seam allowance. Remove the freezer paper right before you fuse each shape.

Shape 1 with fused and paper-backed
Lite Steam-A-Seam 2

3. Remove the paper backing from the Lite Steam-A-Seam 2 on the back of shape 1. Position and fuse shape 1 in place on the muslin foundation.

4. Remove the paper backing from shape 2 and position it so that its seam allowance overlaps the corresponding seam allowance of shape 1; fuse in place.

5. Before adding shape 3, cut a piece of ½"-wide (minimum) trim the length of the seamline between shapes 1 and 2. Using ½" Lite Steam-A-Seam 2, fuse the trim over the seam so that no edges show.

6. Remove the paper backing from the Lite Steam-A-Seam 2 on the back of shape 3, position in place, and fuse. Select your next trim, cut to length, and fuse on top of the seam between shapes 2 and 3, as in Step 5.

Completed block

Prepared shapes, with shape 3 ready to be fused into place

7. Continue adding the next shape and the trim to cover that seam, until all the shapes and trims are fused into place.

8. Zigzag stitch around the perimeter of the fancy fabrics.

9. Mark the finished 8" × 8" perimeter line of the block and sew over the marked line.

Optional: Interface the back of the block with fusible knit interfacing.

10. Sew along the length of both edges of the trim with clear monofilament thread.

After embellishing the block, trim it to 8½" × 8½", which includes ¼" seam allowances (or, if you prefer, to 9" × 9" for ½" seam allowances). Then zigzag stitch around its perimeter before assembling it into a quilt as an 8" × 8" finished block.

❀ METHOD 4
"chunk" piecing

This is, by far, the most random and freewheeling way of constructing a crazy quilt block. However, there is also an element of puzzle solving to it. If you are familiar with the concept of chain piecing, chunk piecing resembles it, at least at first.

Basically you will sew two scraps of fabric right sides together, even if the two scraps are of different shapes and the seam allowances don't line up perfectly (as they must in chain piecing). With chunk piecing, you are just combining scraps, a pair at a time, in one continuous line of sewing. Then cut the pairs apart, press them open, and combine the pairs, two at a time, to create little chunks of pieced fabrics.

The chunks are pressed flat and then fit together on the foundation fabric, with their edges pressed under and appliquéd into place. Additional scraps may be appliquéd to fill in any gaps or holes. As I said, this is very freeform, and it is a fine way to use up those teeny bits of favorite fabric that you just can't throw away. Many thanks to Martha Ellen Green for inspiring me with this method.

In this exercise, we will be making an 8" × 8" finished block.

WHAT YOU'LL NEED

- 10″ × 10″ piece of muslin for the foundation
- Many small scraps of fancy fabrics
- Water-soluble marker or pencil
- 10″ × 10″ piece of knit fusible interfacing (*optional*)
- Clear monofilament thread

1. Mark an 8″ × 8″ square on the foundation muslin.

2. Iron the fabric scraps.

3. Place 2 scraps right sides together and run them through your sewing machine, sewing along one side.

4. Without cutting the threads, run the next pair of scraps through the machine. Continue until you have many pairs; then clip them all apart.

Pairs of randomly seamed scraps: Note that the edges of the scraps do not always line up perfectly. Free-form it is!

5. Press open the pairs. I prefer to press my seams open, but you could also press them to one side. Combine the pairs and run them through the machine again to create chunks. Alternatively, you can add just one scrap of fabric to a pair.

6. Press open the chunks and begin arranging them on the foundation muslin to see how they fit together and what you will need to add to complete your "puzzle."

Scraps in 2-, 3-, and 4-piece chunks, laid out on foundation muslin

7. Make additions to the chunks so that the entire foundation is covered. Press under the edges of each chunk where it overlaps its neighbor and pin them into place.

Chunks pinned on the foundation, ready to be sewn

8. Use clear monofilament thread to appliqué the chunks into place, using a narrow zigzag stitch.

9. Press the block flat and trim off any odd shapes along the perimeter. Zigzag stitch around the perimeter of the fancy fabrics.

10. Mark an 8″ × 8″ square in the center of the block and machine stitch over the marked line.

Optional: Fuse interfacing onto the back of the foundation muslin to prevent fraying.

After embellishing this block, trim it to 8½″ × 8½″, which includes ¼″ seam allowances (or, if you prefer, to 9″ × 9″ for ½″ seam allowances). Then zigzag stitch around its perimeter before assembling it into a quilt as an 8″ × 8″ finished block.

Completed block

Eye Candy: Embellishment!

Now it's time for dessert—and it's a rich one! This chapter is all about eye candy. The basic crazy quilt embroidery stitches and combinations of them, colored lace and trim, the magic element of beads—all go into our confections. In this chapter, you'll also learn to make the three-dimensional flowers that are my personal favorite treat. The ants, spiders, and butterflies that are always attracted to "sweets" will find their way here, too.

Seam treatments and motifs are usually embroidered onto blocks before they are assembled into a quilt. This adds to the portability of crazy quilt stitching that we love so much (like knitting!). However, sometimes you may wish to assemble your whole quilt top before embellishing it—for example, you may plan to carry seam treatments from one block right across to its neighbor. In addition, you can add more seam treatments between the blocks after they are assembled (see the silk ribbon featherstitching between all the blocks in *Crazy in the Desert*, page 65). These are all design decisions you will make as you progress through the making of your quilt.

Tip

Remember that <u>seam treatments</u> refers to embroidery and other embellishments along or over the seams between your block shapes. <u>Motifs</u> are designs within the block shapes.

❧ Classic Crazy Quilt Stitches

These stitches are the basic building blocks of the seam treatments used in crazy quilting. They can be used singly or combined in infinite ways to give a complex and intricate look.

In this section, I provide only a sampling of the many embroidery stitches available. If you're new to embroidery and need to learn the details of these stitches, there are other books and resources that can help you (see the Tip at right).

Tip

For an in-depth look at the intricacies of crazy quilt seam treatments, see the books by Judith Baker Montano that are available from C&T Publishing. For a detailed how-to embroidery guide to hundreds of stitches, Sharon Boggon has developed a comprehensive online stitch dictionary, which she offers for free at <u>www.inaminuteago.com/stitchindex.html</u>. I highly recommend these resources. They both have instructions for lefties, too! Use these resources for detailed information on how to make the stitches called out in this book and for just about any other embroidery stitch.

The embroidery stitch sampler (below) shows some of the basic embroidery stitches used in crazy quilting. All the stitches in the sampler were done in #3 perle cotton. The needle positions show how to make the stitches. A few variations on some of the stitches appear next to and/or below them.

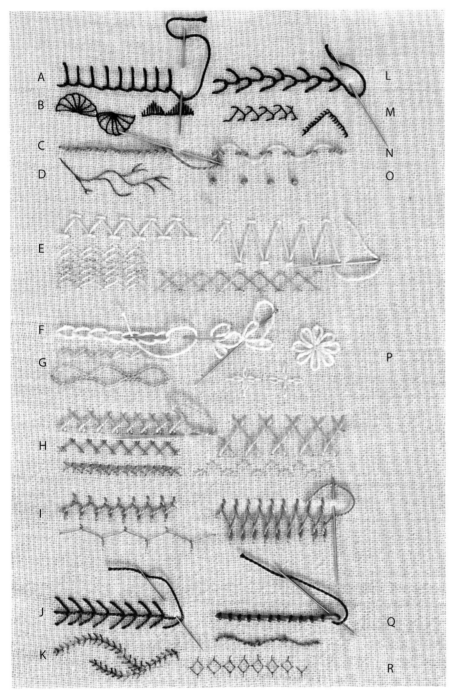

Embroidery stitch sampler

A	Buttonhole
B	Buttonhole wheel and stepped buttonhole
C	Stem
D	Stem variation
E	Chevron and variations
F	Chain
G	Chain variation
H	Herringbone and variations
I	Cretan and variations
J	Fly
K	Fly variation
L	Featherstitch
M	Featherstitch variations
N	Threaded running stitch
O	French knot
P	Detached chain variations
Q	Couching and variation
R	Fly variation

Combining the basic stitches with different colors and threads is one of the most pleasurable aspects of crazy quilting, because each seam is a new adventure in spontaneous design decision making. Sometimes simply weaving contrasting thread through a basically stitched seam treatment can enhance it.

Here are some examples of seam treatments from my work:

Herringbone (worked in 4mm silk ribbon), chevron, and detached chain stitch (detail of *Crazy for Flowers*; full quilt on page 66)

Chevron, straight stitches, and detached chain stitch (detail of *To Mother*; full quilt on page 67)

Double threaded running stitch, chain stitch, and buttonhole wheel (detail of *Crazy for Flowers*; full quilt on page 66)

Chain stitch, detached chain stitch and French knots (detail of *To Mother*; full quilt on page 67)

Buttonhole, fly stitch, and French knots (detail of *Crazy for Flowers*; full quilt on page 66)

Chain stitch stems and detached chain stitch flowers, worked in 4mm silk ribbon (detail of *To Mother*; full quilt on page 67)

Notice how the simple addition of a few beads to the stitches enhances the beauty of the seam treatment. Let's look at some basics of beading on crazy quilts.

🌸 Beads and Other Dimensional Embellishments

Beads and buttons of all types and sizes; crystals, charms, and sequins; pieces of old jewelry; found objects—all add dimension and interest to crazy quilt stitching. You may have been collecting such special treasures for years, knowing they are precious but wondering how and where to use them. Well, this is the place!

Beads and buttons

The variety and types of beads available provide as many design choices as the different kinds of threads do.

The handwork of beading is truly relaxing, and sewing beads onto fabric is quite simple. You do need beading needles, and it is wise to use beading thread, such as Nymo thread, which is much stronger than normal sewing machine thread. You can find these supplies at beading stores. If you wish, you can use a thread conditioner such as beeswax or Thread Heaven, both of which are applied to the thread before threading the needle to prevent fraying or tangling.

While I work, I like to keep the beads I am using on a piece of suede. I find it easy to pick up the beads with the needle, because they don't slide around. Others use linen for this same purpose.

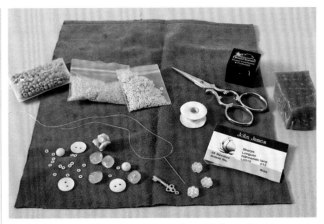

Beads and buttons, thread conditioners (*top right*), needles, Nymo beading thread, and small scissors, all shown here on a suede beading surface

In addition to the basic supplies, all you need to start beading is good light—and perhaps some strong glasses. (I had my optometrist juice up the magnification of the bottom lenses of my trifocals for this very purpose.)

Most of the time, I sew on the beads by coming up through the pieced block with my needle, threading on the bead (or beads), and sewing back down through the block to the back again. Larger beads require going through them a few times, for extra security, just as buttons do. You can also add beads to embroidery stitches *as* you are making them.

Tip

When sewing on bugle beads—the long tubes in the second row of the photo (page 40)—it is good to add a seed bead stopper at either end of each bead. This prevents the glass edges at the ends of the bugle beads from cutting the thread.

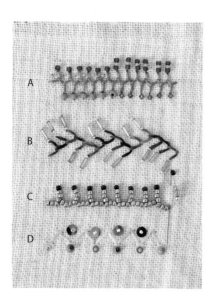

A Seed beads augment a line of embroidery that has a regular pattern. Beads added to cretan stitch create extra interest.

B Bugle and seed beads added to featherstitch

C Seed beads threaded onto embroidery thread and used to create a blanket stitch

D Sequins sewn in place with seed bead stoppers add sparkle and complexity to chevron stitches. (Just come up through the sequin, thread on a seed bead, and go back through the sequin again.)

Flower sequins on a feather stitch and chain stitch shrub. These white butterflies are sequins too!

Beads and buttons used together can add dimension and charm. In the little embellishments sampler (at right), unique buttons were clustered in a grouping. As you can see, you can also add small beads to the surface of a button as you sew it down.

Small or large pressed-glass beads (and buttons) can be integrated into seam treatments and motifs. In the sampler (below), various large beads were perched as flowers atop a row of large buttonhole stitches. The fly stitch was added to create the leaves of the flowers.

Beads can also be used to add texture and line to the interior of crazy quilt shapes. These seed beads almost mimic quilting lines.

This little embellishments sampler features buttons, beads, and embroidery. The narrow green knitting ribbon framing the center image was fused into place and then buttonhole stitched on.

I hope this provides a taste of the wonderful eye candy that beading and buttons can provide to your crazy quilts. The possibilities for delight are endless.

A few beading tips

- If you are sewing a long line of beads along a seam, it is wise to knot off on the back every couple of inches. That way, if your thread should break, the beads won't *all* fall off.

- If you have secured a large bead with a seed bead, and the large bead flops in the wrong direction, use a toothpick to put a tiny dab of E-6000 glue (available at any craft store) on the back; then press the bead into place in the desired position.

- Collect those few extra leftover beads from a beading session in a small lidded tin as "bead soup." You'll have a nice mix to dip into when you need just a bead or two here and there, and you don't want to dig into your bead stash.

Bead soup

❀ Adding Color to Lace, Trim, and Motifs

Laces and premade flowers painted with Liquitex, shown next to their unpainted counterparts

Adding color to lace, trim, and premade ribbon flowers from the craft store is such fun. Some lace comes in the shape of flowers and leaves, which can be cut apart, painted singly, and used in motifs. It's also easy to buy plain white goods and add just that little bit of the exact color you need.

There are several ways to apply pigment, from microwave dyeing with Procion dyes to textile inks and paints. But for me, the simplest way is to use a very thinned-down acrylic paint, such as Liquitex (available from C&T Publishing). It is permanent, it can go on any fiber, and it does not need to be heat set. You can also add some fabric medium to the paint so it will flow more easily and not stiffen the fibers as much when they dry.

Let's try it! Although the following example is a little daisy, you can use this technique with any plain white lace, trim, rickrack, ribbon flowers—whatever you wish to add color to!

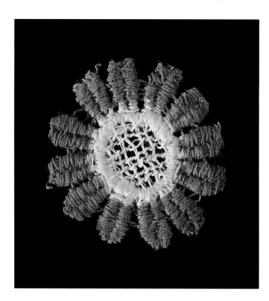

WHAT YOU'LL NEED

- Flower cut from lace

- Liquitex acrylic paints, in a spectrum of colors

- Water-based resist (Jacquard makes a good one.)

- A few small paintbrushes

- A couple of old plates for mixing paint

- Paper towels

- Jar of water

- Sharp embroidery scissors, for cutting apart lace (*optional*)

- Freezer paper laid over newsprint as a painting surface

1. Dampen your flower with water and blot it mostly dry with the paper towel. This will allow the paint to spread smoothly and to be absorbed by all the fibers.

2. Squeeze small amounts of different colors of paint on a plate, leaving room between each. Add some water with a brush to each color and mix, keeping the colors separate or combining them as you like. Rinse and dry the brush in between colors.

3. Squeeze a small amount of resist on the other plate.

4. Using a small amount of the diluted yellow paint, delicately touch the tip of the brush to the center of the flower, filling in the area.

5. Wash your brush in water, dry it on a paper towel, and then use it to paint over the yellow center with the resist. This will help prevent the darker colors from spreading into the center. Rinse and dry the brush.

6. Paint the petals with orange made with a mixture of the red and yellow paints. Paint over the petal tips with magenta, and then with yellow. Let dry.

7. Rinse the resist out of the lace flower, let it dry again, and it is ready to use.

A few painting tips

- Whenever you want to keep areas of color separate, use the resist over the first area you paint before carefully painting the next area.

- You can add some gradient to premade colored flowers to give them more depth: Water down paint and apply it in layers to create shading. I like to go from light to dark rather than from dark to light, because it gives me better control over the finished look. Or you can take white rickrack and make it variegated. Plain guimp trim becomes tonally interesting with different values of the same color.

- Once you are familiar with how easy painting lace and trim can be, you'll find that when you are in the heat of embellishing a block and you realize you need, for example, a few inches of orangey pink lace, you can simply stop and create some!

Remember, these colorful beauties are for crazy quilts, so painting the lace is just the beginning of its transformation!

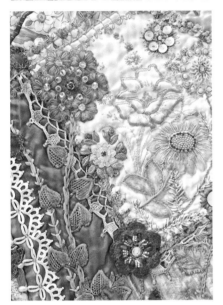

Three details from my small quilt *Queen Allie's Lace* (full quilt on page 63) show how painted doilies, lace, and premade ribbon flowers and leaves look when dressed up with beading and embroidery.

❀ Three-Dimensional Flowers

A bouquet of mixed 3-D blooms

One of my favorite embellishing techniques is to create blooms from ribbon, fabric, and thread. Please remember: All the flowers presented here can be varied however you may wish, depending on what size, type of ribbon, and thread you use. Think of these examples as templates for your own personal blooms.

Embroidered-ribbon dahlia

To make this flower, refer to A Quick Primer on Silk Ribbon Embroidery (page 44). You will stitch the flower on a pieced block or on a piece of background fabric, either of which should be interfaced if you are not using an embroidery hoop.

WHAT YOU'LL NEED

- Pieced block or piece of background fabric

- 4mm silk ribbon in 2 colors—1 light and 1 darker

- Tiny scrap of yellow organza

- Yellow 6-ply embroidery floss

- Plastic mesh circle template (page 18) (This will be used to mark the size of the flower.)

- Needles for silk ribbon and floss embroidery

- Water-soluble marker

- Creative Textile Tool (*optional*)

1. Using the plastic mesh circle guide and a water-soluble pen, mark the middle, inner, and outer concentric circles on the block or background fabric at the size you wish your flower to be.

2. Using the darker color of silk ribbon and a silk ribbon needle, create the outer circle of petals, using the ribbon stitch (A).

3. Use the lighter silk ribbon to create the inner circle of petals as in Step 2, barely overlapping the base of the outer circle's petals (B).

4. Cut out a piece of yellow organza to the size of the innermost circle and pin it to the flower's center.

5. Using the yellow 6-ply embroidery floss, secure the organza center to the flower with 5–7 French knots (see the Tip on page 36). Then separate 3 strands of floss and use it to make a circle of French knots around the perimeter of the flower center (C).

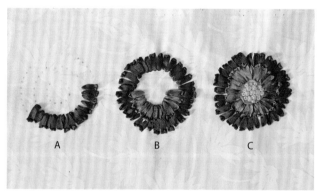

Dahlia in three stages of completion

A quick primer on silk ribbon embroidery (SRE)

Silk ribbon and flowers are a match made in heaven!

To embroider with this ribbon, select a needle with a long, narrow eye to accommodate the ribbon's width. A size #3 crewel embroidery needle works well for 4mm ribbon; for 7mm ribbon, a chenille needle in size #18–#20 is good.

Cut your ribbon no longer than 18". (Some SRE-ers suggest only 12".) To prepare for stitching, thread one end of the cut length of ribbon through the eye of a needle and pull it through far enough so that you can pierce that end with the tip of the needle ½" from the end, as shown. Pull the ribbon snug to lock it into the eye of the needle, so it won't slip out as you stitch.

Basic ribbon stitch

Note: When stitching with silk ribbon, never pull it too tightly. You want to retain the ribbon's fullness.

1. To lock your ribbon to the back of a block without a knot, take a tiny stitch with the ribbon on the back where you wish to begin stitching. Pull most of the way through, pierce the ribbon ½" from the end, and pull the needle through to the front of the fabric.

2. Pull the ribbon away from you so that it lies flat against the fabric. Pierce the ribbon at the length you want the petal to be. Pull the ribbon through to the back, leaving a nice full curl at the tip of the petal. Do not pull too tightly or the curl will disappear! Bring the needle back up through the block to take your next stitch.

3. To end, either lock the ribbon once more on the back or, if you don't have enough ribbon left on your needle (which happens to me all the time), simply bring the ribbon through to the back, secure it with a few stitches of thread, and cut it off.

Gathered ribbon flowers

Detail of *Crazy for Flowers* (full quilt on page 66): This little sweet William was made using three colors of Mokuba ombré ribbon flowers with beads in their centers.

You can gather just about any ribbon or trim of any width to make flowers like this.

Two variations are given here, both using the same principle: The silk ribbon is gathered along one edge, and the gathers are pulled tightly and secured to form the center of the flower, with the ends of the ribbon folded under and then sewn closed. The flower is anchored to the pieced block or background fabric with a few stitches.

VARIATION 1

For this version, you'll need a short length of 7mm silk ribbon (6″ long for this example) and some fine silk sewing thread.

1. Thread a fine needle with 18″ of silk thread. Knot the end and clip off any extra thread beyond the knot.

2. Cut the ribbon to 5″ long and fold back one end ½″. With a threaded needle, take a stitch up from the back of the fold through both layers to the front of the ribbon near one edge. Begin making a line of running stitches along one edge (A).

3. Continue the running stitch, using small stitches, along the edge of the ribbon to within 1″ of the other end. Fold that end back ½″ as well and continue the running stitch through both layers to the fold (B).

4. Set aside this needle but keep it threaded. Form a circle with the ribbon by bringing both folded ends alongside each other, pinched together in your nonsewing hand. With your other hand, pull the thread to gather the ribbon.

5. Keeping the ribbon tightly gathered, take a couple of small stitches at the base where the 2 folds meet; then make a small knot to secure the gathers.

6. Whipstitch the folds closed to complete the flower. Knot off (C).

7. Attach the flower to the background with a few tiny stitches around the perimeter (D). The center can be filled with a bead, French knots, straight stitches, or whatever you like.

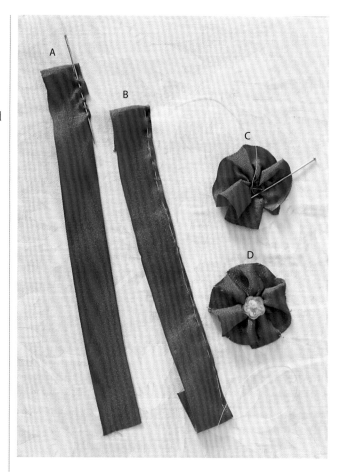

VARIATION 2

Ombré picot ribbon makes the cutest gathered ribbon flowers. (Ombré, also called rainbow ribbon, refers to the graduations between colors or between the values of one color; picot ribbon features looped edges.) You can get two different effects with this ribbon, depending on whether you place the dark-colored or light-colored edge in your flower center. Mokuba (see Suppliers, page 127) makes a wonderful woven rayon ombré picot ribbon.

For this flower, you will need a way to seal one of the ribbon's cut edges. The fine point of the Creative Textile Tool is ideal for this technique (see Suppliers, page 127). Or you can very carefully pass the cut end about ½″ above a candle flame until it melts. *Important: Please hold the ribbon in a tweezers for this to keep your fingers safe, and keep a jar of water nearby!*

For this variation, you'll need a 2″ length of ¼″ Mokuba woven rayon ombré ribbon, some fine silk sewing thread, and, if you want to use it, the Creative Textile Tool.

1. Thread a fine needle with silk thread and knot the end.

2. Cut and seal one end of the ribbon. Measure 1½″ and cut the other end with sharp scissors (A).

3. On the scissor-cut end, find a thread in the warp of the ribbon along the light-colored edge. Because the other end is sealed, you will be able to pull this as your gathering thread. Go ahead and pull (B)! After the ribbon is gathered, pinch it in your nonsewing hand between thumb and forefinger.

4. Fold under the scissor-cut end and whipstitch it in place, just overlapping the sealed edge, to create a flower. Secure it to the background with a few whipstitches (C).

For a different look from the same ribbon, gather the darker edge (D).

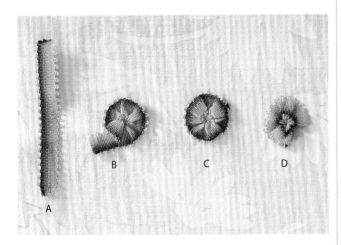

Wire-edged ribbon bellflowers

Detail of bellflowers from *Crazy Happy Flowers*
(full quilt on page 109)

There are so many ways to use this kind of ribbon. Its hidden wires along each edge enable you to shape the ribbon. And yet I always seem to use it to make my beloved bellflowers.

Here, we'll make a bellflower with leaf and stem. You will stitch the flower on a pieced block or on a piece of background fabric, either of which should be interfaced if you are not using an embroidery hoop.

WHAT YOU'LL NEED

- Pieced block or background fabric

- 1½″-wide wired ribbon, about 5″ long per bell, or 6″–7″ long for a full, ruffly bell

- 1″-wide green wired ribbon, about 6″ long per leaf (I tend to prefer ombré ribbon for these, but solid-colored wired ribbon works fine as well.)

- 7mm green silk ribbon, about 14″ long per bell, for the stem

- Fine green thread and needle

- Large ribbon crewel needle

- Not your best scissors!
  (You will be cutting through fine wire, after all.)

~Bell~

Refer to the photo at right.

1. Cut a 5″ length from the 1½″ ribbon. Fold in half crosswise.

2. To gather the ribbon, very carefully find and grasp the wires on each end of the light edge of the ribbon. Pinch the wire ends together in one hand, while sliding the ribbon toward the center fold along the wire to gather it. When you can't push the gathers any tighter, twist the 2 wires together a few times to secure the gathers. Trim off any little fraying threads and clip the wires to ½″ (A).

3. Fold back one end of the ribbon to hide the raw edge. Then place the other end of the ribbon behind it. Pin in place on the background fabric (B).

4. Shape your ribbon flower as desired and pin it, tucking the wire ends behind the bell. Shape a little scalloped edge along the front of the bell. Appliqué the bell in place, going around the bell and removing pins as you go. Keep the scalloped edge in front free.

5. Make a calyx with the 7mm green silk ribbon to cover the bottom edge of the bell (E). Using a large ribbon crewel needle, take a few basic ribbon stitches (pages 44–45).

~Leaf~

1. This time, do not cut the ribbon before gathering an end, because it is too easy to lose the other end of the wire when you are gathering from just one end. Instead, simply find the wire on the light end of your ribbon and begin pushing the ribbon into gathers, sliding the ribbon down the wire (C).

2. Fold the ribbon as shown to form both sides of the leaf, gathered edges touching. Fold under the bottom and side edges of the ribbon ends to the back, twisting them a little bit. *Then* cut off any excess ribbon and pin into place (D).

3. Appliqué the leaf to the background, whipstitching the center vein closed, if desired.

~Stem~

1. With the 7mm green silk ribbon threaded in a large ribbon needle, bring the ribbon up through the block where the bottom end of the stem will be.

2. Twist the ribbon to form the stem.

3. Bring the twisted ribbon to the back of the block at the base of the calyx.

4. Gently couch the twisted ribbon stem into place with fine silk thread. Don't pull too tightly (E).

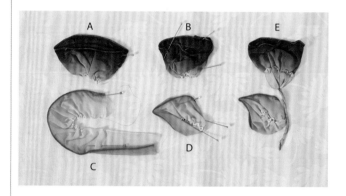

Folded ribbon rosebud

Detail of *At 17* (full quilt on page 64). A spray of folded rosebuds with featherstitching and French knots.

Detail of a floral sampler block made by the author. Rosebuds made from wire-edged ribbon with silk ribbon calyxes.

As with all the flowers presented here, you can vary the folded rosebud in many ways. You can make large versions using very wide ribbon or teeny ones using ½″-wide ribbon. The rosebuds presented here fall somewhere in the middle. You will create and stitch the flower on a pieced block or on a piece of background fabric, either of which should be interfaced if you are not using an embroidery hoop.

WHAT YOU'LL NEED

- 1″-wide silk ribbon, 6″ in length per bud, folded and ironed in half lengthwise

- Green wool embroidery thread

- #8 green silk perle

- Strong sewing or beading thread to match the ribbon

- Fine needle

1. Thread the needle with sewing thread and knot the end.

2. To form the bud, before attaching it to the background, place the ribbon vertically and fold the top end at a 45° angle to form a triangle (A).

3. Fold up the long right end of the ribbon. Wrap the ribbon around the back of the triangle and then down toward the bottom again, like a little shawl. Pin (but not to the background fabric yet). Take a few stitches at the center bottom to hold the folds in place (B).

4. Fold the ribbon back and around the other way (opposite of how it was done in Step 3). Take a tiny stitch at the fold where the ribbon comes around from the back (C). The ribbon should now hang down on the right side.

5. Make 1 or 2 stitches through all layers at the bud's center base. Then make a running stitch through all layers along the bottom edge, just below where the ribbons cross at the bottom (not shown). Pull the thread to gather along the base, wrap the thread around the gathered base a few times, and knot off. Carefully snip any excess ribbon off the base a scant ¼″ from the stitching. Wrap the stump with a few additional stitches to make it more compact (D).

6. Now, attach the bud to the background fabric using hidden stitches at the sides and the tip.

7. For the calyx at the base of the bud, use green wool to make straight stitches that cover the stump's raw edges.

8. For the stem, double the silk perle and stem stitch (page 37) up to the base of the calyx (E).

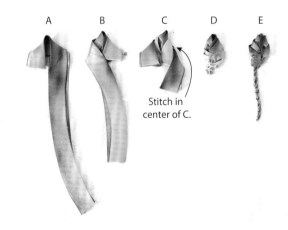

A   B   C   D   E

Stitch in center of C.

Rickrack yarrow flower

Detail of *Crazy in the Garden* (full quilt on page 5). Note the ¼″ rickrack for the left-side dark flower, ⅛″ (3mm) rickrack for the smaller right flower, and leaves made with a buttonhole stitch (page 37).

My favorite flowers of this kind are made from narrow rayon rickrack just 3mm wide. Mokuba makes a good rickrack for this use (see Suppliers, page 127). This flower requires using two different needles at once—one threaded with the rickrack, and the other with strong, fine thread. But this is not hard once you get the hang of it.

You'll create these flowers directly on your pieced block or background fabric, either of which should be interfaced if you are not using an embroidery hoop.

Detail of *Crazy Happy Flowers* (full quilt on page 109). A tiny spray of folded rosebuds using ½″-wide silk ribbon.

WHAT YOU'LL NEED

- A few 18″ lengths of 3mm rayon rickrack
- Needle large enough to accommodate the rickrack
- Beading thread to match the rickrack
- Fine needle
- Green cotton or silk floss
- Embroidery needle
- Pliers (optional)
- Water-soluble marking pen

1. To indicate where each flower will be placed, mark the fabric with dots spaced about ½″ apart. They should form 2 parallel curved lines, with 5 dots on the top line and 6 on the bottom line.

2. Thread 18″ of rickrack onto a large needle and bring it to the front from the back, through the first marked dot. Use pliers to pull it through if necessary. Leave a ½″ tail on the back. Set the needle down.

3. Thread the fine needle with beading thread, knot it, and stitch the tail of the rickrack to the back of the fabric. Bring the needle to the front, next to the rickrack.

4. Sew the rickrack onto the same fine needle by going in and out along the tops of the V's until you have 12 V's on your needle. Pull the thread through to gather the rickrack, forming a little flower. Make a tiny knot into the base of the flower to secure the gathers.

5. Take the large needle threaded with rickrack to the back again, right next to the base of the little flower, using pliers if necessary. Pull it snug. Then set the large needle down and use the fine thread to take a few stitches to shape your rickrack flower and secure it to the background fabric. Bring the beading thread to the back again and knot it off. Do not cut the fine thread; just set the needle down.

6. Carry the rickrack across the back ½″ and come up through the next dot. Bring the fine needle to the front of the piece next to the rickrack (A). Repeat Steps 4 and 5.

7. Complete all 11 flowers in this way. Clip off excess rickrack and secure the last tail end on the back with the fine thread.

8. Draw lines from the flowers to a point ⅝″ below the center of the bottom row of flowers. Mark the stem and the center line of the leaf.

9. Sew 3 strands of green floss in a straight stitch to cover the lines from the flowers to the point.

10. Use a stem stitch (page 37) for the stem and a fly stitch (page 37) for the leaf (B).

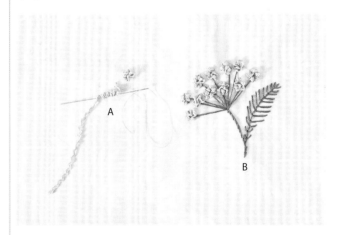

Angelina lilac

Because Angelina fused to light silk does not ravel when it is cut (for more on Angelina, see page 24), it is the perfect material for making three-dimensional flowers. In the lilac shown (pages 31 and 32), the little blooms are held on by the beads in their centers, with the petals remaining free. The leaf uses wool and silk roving, needle felted onto cotton, for the same reason—it won't fray when cut. Wool felt is an excellent alternative here. The leaf is attached with a beaded buttonhole stitch.

Angelina can be used to create just about any flower you like, especially flowers with petal shapes that would be too small or irregularly shaped to appliqué. So you can apply this floral concept all around your "garden."

Here, you will stitch the flowers on a pieced block or on a piece of background fabric, either of which should be interfaced if you are not using an embroidery hoop.

WHAT YOU'LL NEED

- Pieced block or background fabric
- Small amount of Angelina fibers, fused into a sheet and then fused to lightweight silk—enough to make a 5″ × 5″ square
- Small piece of wool felt
- Green #8 perle in linen, cotton, or silk
- Green silk floss
- Size 11 green seed beads
- Size 15 yellow seed beads
- Beading needle and thread
- Embroidery needle
- Water-soluble marker

1. Rough cut 16 squares ¾″ × ¾″ from the Angelina/silk square. Freehand cut a 4-petal flower from each little square.

2. Mark the stem and leaf placement on the background fabric or block.

3. Use #8 perle in a stem stitch (page 37) to create the main stem of the flower cluster. Use a single straight stitch where the flowers connect to the main stem.

4. Cut a heart-shaped leaf from the felt and pin it into place. Using a single strand of the silk floss in a beading needle, blanket stitch (page 37) around the leaf. Add a seed bead to the needle before taking each stitch (A). Using a stem stitch, embroider the veins on the leaf.

5. Thread a beading needle with beading thread. Attach the flowers to the background fabric or block one at a time by coming up through the Angelina fabric, piercing the flower, and threading on first a green and then a yellow seed bead. Go back down through the green bead to the back and move on to the next flower. Place the flowers so that a bit of the little stems show through (B).

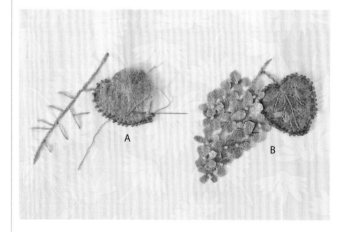

A variation on this flower is the wild rose made from Angelina in this detail of *Crazy in the Garden* (full quilt on page 5). The white in the center of the petals was added with colored pencil. Straight stitching, along with the beads in the rose centers, helps secure the petals to the quilt. The silk chiffon leaves were attached simply by running a stem stitch (page 37) down their centers.

Rose

Detail of *Crazy in the Garden* (full quilt on page 5). Some of these are vintage millinery flowers, and some are roses I made using the method described here. Can you tell which are which?

This rose is constructed before it is sewn onto the block or background fabric. It is the most *involved* of the flowers here, but it is worth every step. I've created my own petals, but you can purchase some ready-made petals in the bridal section of a craft store. I do use purchased tiny wired paper roses for the centers of my flowers, because of the convenience of being able to stitch into them as I build my roses. The floral wire is also handy for helping attach the rose when it is done.

WHAT YOU'LL NEED

- Pieced block or background fabric

- 12″ × 16″ white synthetic lightweight fabric (I used white lining material.)

- Small bunch of very small wire-stemmed paper roses

- 1″ × 1″ square of green Ultrasuede and a large needle for poking a hole in it

- Pink Liquitex paint

- Paintbrush

- Water

- Plate for mixing paint

- Creative Textile Tool with fine-point tip (*optional; see Suppliers, page 127*)

- Heatproof surface (*optional*)

- Beading thread

- Fine needle

- Fabric glue

- Iron

1. From the white synthetic fabric, cut out the petals, using the photo (at right) as a guide. You can use the Creative Textile Tool (on a heatproof surface) to cut out and heat seal the petals, or you can cut them out with scissors and seal their edges over a candle flame, as described in Gathered Ribbon Flowers (page 46). *Hold them with tweezers and use caution!* Cut out 18 petals per rose, graduating from 1″–2″ in size.

2. On a plate, thin out a small amount of pink paint with water. Paint the base of the petals with the pink wash, letting it fade to white at the top of the petals. Allow the petals to dry.

3. To give the petals a slight curve, place the tip of a heated iron, set to "silk," in the center of a petal while pulling up on the top edge. This will curl the fabric petal. Watch those fingers!

4. Separate 1 wire-stemmed paper rose from the bunch. Peel off the green paper calyx. Thread a needle with beading thread and knot off.

5. Sew the first petal to the base of the paper rose, going through the paper rose. Attach the second petal to the opposite side, again sewing through the base of the paper rose. Continue with 2 more petals (A).

6. Keep adding petals, using larger ones as you go around the base of the rose. Take some extra stitches as required to position the petals evenly, wrapping thread around the base to keep the petals snug. Continue until all the petals are in place. Wrap any remaining thread around the base of the rose, where the wire comes out. Knot off. Your rose should look nice and full (B).

7. From the green Ultrasuede, cut out a calyx (C), using the photo (below) as a guide. With the large needle, poke a hole in the center of the calyx. Smear fabric glue on the back and thread it onto the rose's wire, glue side up. Slide it up to the petals and pinch it into place. Let dry.

8. To attach the rose to fabric, poke a hole in the fabric with the large needle and feed the wire through to the back. Secure the wire with a few tiny stitches on the back. There is your full and lovely rose! (D) You may add a stem if desired, of course.

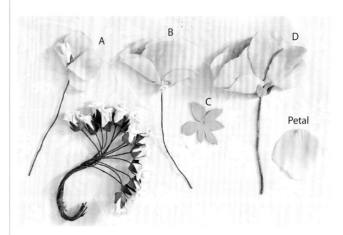

Beaded button flower

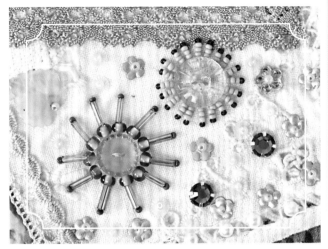

Bugle bead/button flower used on *"Sisters" Crazy Quilt Scrapbook Page* (full quilt on page 88)

There are innumerable ways to combine buttons and beads to make whimsical flowers. These beaded button flowers are a great way to use the odd buttons from your collection, and you don't need many beads. Here, we'll make one flower, constructed directly on the block or background fabric (either interface it or use an embroidery hoop).

WHAT YOU'LL NEED

- Pieced block or background fabric
- ½"-diameter button
- Size 13 seed beads in light, medium, and dark blue
- Beading thread
- Size 11 beading needle
- Plastic mesh circle template (page 18)
- Water-soluble marker

1. Using the template, mark a circle of 20 dots with about a 1¼" diameter where you wish your flower to go on the block or background fabric.

2. Sew the button in the center of the marked circle.

3. Bring the beading needle up from the back at the edge of the button. Thread on seed beads—2 light blue, 1 medium blue, and then 1 dark blue.

4. Bring the needle down at the marked dot above the spot where you brought the needle up. Pull the beads snugly into position.

5. Take your next stitch beside the first row of beads, along the edge of the button; repeat Steps 3 and 4.

6. Complete the button flower with a total of 20 petals. Knot off the thread.

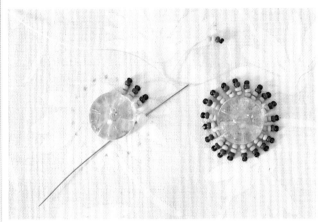

✿ Butterflies, Spiders, and Ants

A silk-winged butterfly; a juicy, creepy spider; and a parade of ants—soon you may have them crawling all over your crazy quilts!

Butterflies are our beloved petals of the wind. There are as many ways to create a butterfly as there are to create a flower. To get you started, I present just one example, using embroidered silk and beads.

As for bugs, I never liked them until I became a crazy quilter. Traditionally, spiders were included on early crazy quilts as a symbol of good luck. So, wanting to keep with tradition, I made my first spider. It was so much fun … and kind of creepy! Afterward, I started studying them as I came across them in my garden, and now I love them.

Those ants have a hill in my garden that they've maintained for 18 years, so I've learned to love and render them, too.

All of these little creatures are sewn directly onto background fabric or a block, either of which should be interfaced if you are not using an embroidery hoop.

Butterfly

Wing patterns are on page 57.

WHAT YOU'LL NEED

- Pieced block or background fabric

- Small scraps of lightweight silk

- Kreinik #8 fine metallic thread and needle for wing embroidery

- 2 long bugle beads, 1 large round bead, and a few #11 seed beads for the body

- 16 #11 seed beads for the antenna

- Beading needle and thread

- Candle, matches, and tweezers *(optional)*

- Temporary adhesive spray *(optional)*

1. Trace the 4 wing patterns onto tracing paper and use them to cut out the silk.

Tip

If you wish, you can burn the edges of the silk wing shapes to prevent fraying and create a nice black outline. Hold the wing with a pair of tweezers and <u>quickly</u> pass the edges over the top of a candle flame. Don't let the silk catch fire! (Thank you to Victoria Adams Brown for teaching me this technique.)

2. If desired, spray the backs of the wing pieces very lightly with adhesive spray. (This helps keep the "floaty" silk in place while you embroider it.) Smooth the wings into position on the block or fabric. Otherwise, pin the wing shapes in place.

3. Using Kreinik metallic thread in a fly stitch (page 37), embroider the top and bottom wing parts.

4. Sew on the 2 bugle beads to create the butterfly's body. Add the large round bead directly above it. Come back through the round bead, thread on 8 small seed beads, and sew to the left for an antenna. Repeat for the right side. Add a few beads at the base of the body.

Spider

WHAT YOU'LL NEED

- Pieced block or background fabric

- 1 pear-shaped bead

- 1 crystal (4mm)

- 16 bugle beads

- 24 #15 seed beads

- 2 #11 seed beads

- Beading needle and thread

1. Sew the pear-shaped bead for the abdomen onto the block or fabric.

2. Bring your needle back through the bead, add the crystal for the prosoma (looks like a head, but with legs on the sides) and sew it down.

3. Coming back through the crystal, add both of the #11 seed beads for the eyes and come back down through the crystal the other way. Make a small stitch over the threads going into the crystal from the seed beads, and couch them down (page 37).

4. For your spider to look realistic, all the legs must originate from the sides of the prosoma. For each leg, bring the thread up next to the crystal and string on a #15 seed bead, a bugle bead, another seed bead, another bugle bead, and then a third seed bead. Bring the needle to the back. Repeat for all 8 legs, arranging them around the spider.

Ants

WHAT YOU'LL NEED (for each ant)

- Pieced block or background fabric
- 1 small nailhead bead (flat on one side, rounded on the other)
- 1 small bugle bead
- 1 #11 seed bead
- Beading needle and black beading thread

1. Sew the nailhead bead for the abdomen onto the background fabric.

2. Bring your needle back through the nailhead. Add a bugle bead for the thorax and a seed bead for the head. Sew them down, keeping all the beads in a straight line.

3. Use black beading thread to embroider 6 legs, all emerging from the thorax (the bugle bead). What makes a leg look "antlike" is its 3 joints, so try to use 3 short straight stitches per leg.

4. Come back through the ant's head and create the antenna with a straight stitch. Repeat for the second antenna.

You can purchase wonderful cloisonné spiders and butterflies as well. In this detail of *To Mother* (full quilt on page 67), the painted-lace-and-beaded butterfly escaped from the web, but the cloisonné butterfly was not so lucky. I call this my "PMS spiderweb."

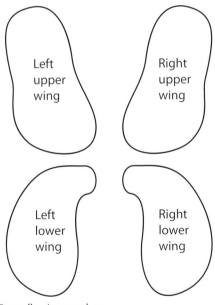

Left upper wing

Right upper wing

Left lower wing

Right lower wing

Butterfly wing templates

Gallery of Inspiration

"Inspired by antique crazy quilt fans in my collection, I had to make one myself," says Betty. "It is completely hand stitched and embroidered."

Crazy Quilting: I'm a Fan, 25″ × 17″, by Betty Pillsbury, 2005

*L*ike other quiltmaking genres, crazy quilts are evolving. New technologies and supplies are certainly a factor in this evolution, but I think the deeper reason is the increased freedom each quiltmaker feels in exploring his or her own interpretation of what crazy quilting means.

The parameters of what makes a crazy quilt, well, crazy, are still in evidence: the juxtaposition of various fabrics, some randomness to the piecing, embellishment along the seams and within the shapes of fabrics, the absence of quilting. But any crazy quilter will tell you that our motto is "No rules!" Some of the quilts presented here do break a few rules, in that they do not fall within all of the above parameters. But overall, I believe that their beauty, strength, and interest lie in their ability to stretch the notion of what crazy quilting can be. Other quilts shown here are traditional, and they show what incredible results come from extended commitment to and focus on fine handwork in the time-honored genre of crazy quilting.

I am so pleased to be able to share the incredible work of my fellow stitchers with you. Come feast your eyes....

"References to traditional crazy quilting and historical textiles are in this quilt," Sharon says. *"The diamond shapes of the blocks were inspired by an Australian crazy quilt made by Martha Bingley in 1883. Every block contains paisley prints. Since the paisley pattern is Persian in origin and represents the growing shoot of a date palm, it has become associated with the tree of life. The quilt references this, as I took the idea and applied a contemporary garden theme to the quilt. So floral motifs, dragonflies, butterflies and the traditional spiderweb for good luck are all to be found in the blocks."*

Crazy Diamonds, 56″ × 70″, by Sharon Boggon, 2009

Detail of *Crazy Diamonds*

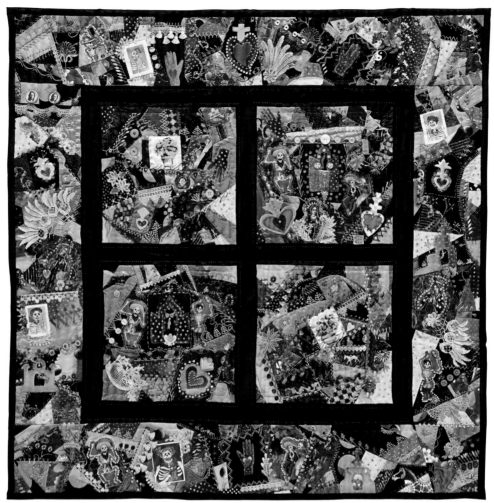

New Mexico, 42½" × 42½", by Martha Green, 2006

The Carney Roadside School of Crazy Quilting has been beloved by Martha's students all over the world. Her take on crazy quilting is "out of the box," for sure. About this quilt she says, "I try to get out to New Mexico at least once a year to paint and visit friends. I always come back a little enchanted, so this quilt is a result of bathing in the afterglow of a trip to Santa Fe. Having a detailed design or plan is really contrary to the nature of crazy quilting. I limit my decision making, but sometimes settle on a theme or color scheme. Crazy quilts are little emotional road maps, and for me, it's best that I chart a very undefined course and get out of the way.

"I had drawn some skeleton ladies on the computer and transferred them to cloth. I wanted them to have a nice place to live, so that was a starting point for the quilt. I wanted the piece to be reminiscent of Fiesta, the Day of the Dead celebration, and to reflect the nature of New Mexico culture. For a spiritual and magical aspect, I included the milagros, both constructed and real. I also wanted it to be an infinity trap, so I continued with churches, more skeletons, and altars with Madonnas.

"Unlike sane quilting, which is all about precision, crazy quilting is about your mind, your heart, and your hands. We feel our way through a project, using our senses rather than a ruler."

My Favorite Things, 60″ × 60″, by Debra Spincic, 2009

Debra says, "This quilt is an explorative work combining machine and hand embroidery in a contemporary crazy quilt format. When I discovered that I could embroider cross-stitch designs by machine, I used that process as the basis of My Favorite Things. Other machine-embroidery techniques were added to flesh out the idea that hand and machine embroidery can harmoniously complement each other in a composition."

Detail of *My Favorite Things*

"I have an attraction to both vintage linens and old holy card images," says Barbara. "I chose a household item and a personal item—a tea towel and a hankie—as foundations for a crazy quilt featuring St. Therese of Lisieux, the 'little flower.' I wanted to mirror her insight that there is grace in the simple and the everyday. The rose motifs in both items were serendipitous and directed my approach to embellishing this quilt. In her spiritual writings, St. Therese reflected, 'The only way I can prove my love is by scattering flowers, and these flowers are every little sacrifice, every glance and word, and the doing of the least actions for love.'"

Little Flower, 18″ × 29″, by Barbara Curiel, 2008

Detail of *Little Flower*

Queen Allie's Lace, 20″ × 20″, by the author, 2004

A Modern Romance, 16″ × 16″, by Debra Jo Hardman, 2009

Debra actually constructed and quilted this piece on her longarm machine. Then she drew from her vast repertoire of needlework techniques to embellish this groundbreaking crazy quilt. This is the best integration of machine quilting with crazy quilting that I have ever seen.

The seam treatments for this quilt were created using waste canvas, as shown in Use Waste Canvas (page 17).

At 17, 8″ × 8″, by the author, 2008

Crazy in the Desert, 58″ × 72″, by the author, 2002

*This quilt started it all for me. My excitement at working with new fabrics,
beads, and techniques knew no bounds. It took almost a year to make.*

Crazy for Flowers, 49″ × 59″, by the author, 2006

This was the first time I used three-dimensional flowers on a crazy quilt. It was a totally joyous experience for me. To see a detail from this quilt, see pages 2 and 3.

For Uncle Hal, with Love, 40″ × 40″, by the author, 2008

"H," my father's younger brother, became very dear to me during the last years of his life. This tribute to him was my way of grieving his loss. My goal as a quiltmaker was to combine a sense of tradition with a contemporary feel ... just as H did himself.

My homage to the maternal is in this quilt—to our Victorian mothers who began the needle art of crazy quilting, to Mother Nature who inspires us in our work, and to the great gift that motherhood has been in my own life (the initials in the corners are for myself, my husband, and my two sons).

To Mother, 53″ × 53″, by the author, 2003

Summer Lake Day, 62″ × 71″, by the author, 2003

I tried to combine my new love of crazy quilting and my old love of landscape
quilting in this piece, which depicts abstract as well as representational imagery.

Marty says, "'Where oxlips and the nodding violet grows ... With sweet musk-roses and with eglantine: There sleeps Titania sometime of the night.' These words from Shakespeare's A Midsummer Night's Dream were the inspiration for this quilt. Queen Titania sleeping in her bower was painted by my son, Nat Trahan, and I designed the remainder of the quilt around this scene. The viewer, joined by snails, snakes, and spiders, peeks through the grasses on the border to see Titania. Joined by her ever-watchful fairies, she sleeps peacefully and waits for Oberon."

Detail of *One Midsummer Night* bottom border

One Midsummer Night, 42" × 62", by Marty Trahan, 2010

My Hardworking, Honed-by-Experience
Needle Cushion

Designed and made by the author.   Finished size: approximately 9″ × 5″

WHAT YOU'LL NEED

- 18″ × 14″ *loosely woven* muslin or other foundation fabric

- 9 large scraps of woven wool for the needle cushion top

- 2 strips of fabric 10″ × 4″ and 2 strips of fabric 4″ × 12″ for the bottom*

- 1 yard of rickrack or other trim

- Small round beads

- 3-ply wool tapestry yarn (like the kind used in needlepoint) in 15–20 colors

- About 2½ ounces of wool roving

- 9″ × 5″ piece of foamcore or heavy corrugated cardboard

- Strong sewing thread, such as hand quilting or beading thread

*I chose a border print and used the colors in it as the palette inspiration for my embroidery colors.

NOTE: This block has no fusible interfacing backing it. Interfacing would interfere with the ease of inserting the needles into the cushion.

*O*nce you get engrossed in a crazy quilting project, you will need many different kinds and sizes of needles. I like mine easy to see, grab, and put back, with many of them threaded and ready to go.

This needle cushion project is the result of years of road testing. The fabrics and threads are all wool, because it is easy to jam a needle in and out of wool while in the heat of stitching. For the same reason, I used wool roving for the stuffing. The shape is long and rectangular, so you can fit a whole bunch of needles in it at once, even keeping the fine ones at one end and the fat ones at the other. Although it includes pretty wool stitching, it has no 3-D motifs to get in the way.

Think of what it means to have a really great tool belt if you are a carpenter or a fantastic knife rack if you are a chef. That's what this needle cushion is to this crazy quilter!

8

9

7

6

2

1

3

4

5

❧ Piece the Needle Cushion

I recommend straight-edge foundation piecing (page 27) for constructing this block.

1. Using the block diagram (page 72) as a guide, make a full-size pattern for the pieced top of the needle cushion. The lines shown are the finished seamlines. Trace this pattern onto the muslin. When cutting the wool pieces, remember to add seam allowances and to have extra fabric extend beyond the finished block perimeter line. Follow the piecing sequence on the block diagram to piece the wool scraps.

2. On the pieced block, draw a 10″ × 6″ rectangle to mark the perimeter of the cushion's top. (Note: ½″ seam allowances are included within the area of this marked rectangle.) A white gel pen and a white chalk marker work equally well on wool.

3. Using the perimeter marked lines as a guide and with ½″ seam allowances all around, sew the 10″ × 4″ strips to the top and bottom (long edges) of the marked rectangle. Press. Sew the 4″ × 12″ strips to the sides and press. Trim the seam allowances to ¼″. Zigzag stitch around the outside edges of the attached border strips. Trim the muslin even with the outside edges of the border strips.

Needle cushion block with borders, ready to embellish

❧ Embellish the Top

For various embroidery stitches, see the embroidery stitch sampler (page 37) and refer to the tip on crazy quilt seam treatments (page 36).

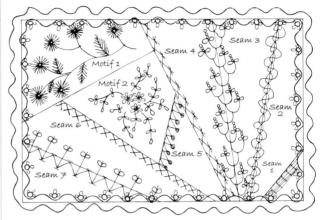

Embellishment diagram

Referring to the embellishment diagram, complete the following seams and motifs with wool yarn.

Seams

Seam 1   1-ply blue yarn in a blanket stitch along the seam; 3-ply gray yarn woven through the vertical stitches (Use the eye end of the needle to weave.)

Seam 2   1-ply blue yarn in a chain stitch along the seam; 1-ply maroon yarn woven in and out of the chain stitches

Seam 3   3-ply green yarn in a large featherstitch for the stems along both sides of the seam; 1-ply green in a single detached chain stitch for the leaves; 1-ply light green in a smaller detached chain stitch in the leaf centers; 3 French knots (4-wrap) in 1-ply pink, red, and maroon, above the leaf centers

Seam 4   1-ply blue yarn in a herringbone stitch along one side of the seam; 1-ply gray yarn in a straight stitch at each upper cross

Seam 5   1-ply olive green yarn in a slanted long-and-short blanket stitch; 1-ply lighter green yarn in a straight stitch between vertical blanket stitches; a single detached chain stitch in 1-ply yellow at the top of each straight stitch; a 2-wrap French knot in 1-ply green in the center of each chain stitch

Seam 6   1-ply pink yarn (2 shades) in cross-stitches along the seam

Seam 7   3-ply olive green yarn in a chevron stitch along one seam edge; 1-ply lighter green in a long straight stitch for the stems extending above the chevrons and in a single fly stitch at the top of each stem; 1-ply pink yarn for 2 detached chain stitches above the fly stitches; 1-ply darker pink in single straight stitches to fill the detached chain stitches; 1-ply red in a short straight stitch between the sets of detached chain stitches

Motifs

MOTIF 1

Curved stems   2-ply green yarn in a stem stitch

Flowers   1-ply yarn in light and medium blue, with 10 straight stitches in each color

Flower centers   1-ply yellow yarn in a 3-wrap French knot

Leaves   1-ply lighter green yarn in a fly stitch

MOTIF 2

Curved stems   1-ply medium green yarn in a stem stitch

Leaves   1-ply lighter green yarn in single detached chain stitches; fill each with 1-ply dark green yarn in a straight stitch

Flowers   1-ply yellow yarn in 6 detached chain stitches each; fill in the petals with smaller detached chain stitches

Flower centers   1-ply red yarn in a 3-crossing straight stitch

Attach the rickrack or trim of your choice around the wool pieced block. You can either use a sewing machine and zigzag with a clear thread or appliqué it on by hand. In between each "dip" in the rickrack, make a fly stitch on the wool pieced block with a detached chain stitch in the center. I used a light silk thread for this, but you could use more wool. Sew a bead at the base of each fly stitch.

❧ Finish the Needle Cushion

1. Place the embellished block facedown on a flat surface. Arrange the wool roving so that it evenly covers the pieced wool portion. Center the piece of foamcore over the roving.

2. Fold the side strips to the back, over the foamcore (there will be a gap on the back between their edges). Using a strong sewing thread, lace these 2 edges together across the back of the foamcore, pulling very snugly to pack the roving. See How to Mount Your Small Quilt Top onto Foamcore (page 87) for more information. Make sure the rickrack along the rectangle's side edges is aligned with the edges of the foamcore. For a project this size, space the laces about ½" apart and take a bite of about ½" into the backing strips to ensure that they won't fray under the tension.

3. Fold the bottom strip to the back and secure in place by vertically pinning directly into the foamcore from the back. Fold the top strip to the back, turning under the zigzagged edge. Pin into place by vertically pinning through all layers, directly into the foamcore. Make adjustments, folding and stretching the fabric and repinning as necessary, until the rickrack is perfectly aligned along the edges of the foamcore and the block is quite snug.

4. Whipstitch all pinned edges closed with a strong thread, removing the vertical pins as you go.

Your needle cushion is complete and ready for action! Of course, you could also use this for pins....

Floral Sampler

Designed and made by the author, 2009.   Finished size: 17″ × 17″

*T*his little quilt gives you a great chance to play with some flower and bug embellishment ideas from Eye Candy: Embellishment! (page 36). You will start by piecing the center block and inner border. Next you will embroider the seams on the block, and then you will add the flowers and bugs. Although a complete embellishment diagram and instructions for this piece are given, I encourage you to vary them as you wish to create your own version of this little garden.

The interesting coloration and finished edges of ombré wire-edged ribbons offer such nice possibilities for finishing little quilts like this. Here I have appliquéd wire-edged ribbon to the front of the quilt to function as the outer border; the backing of the quilt is simply whipstitched to the ribbon's outer edge. This finishing technique is simple, fast, and functional, but adds a lot of bang for your buck. I'm all for that … always.

WHAT YOU'LL NEED

Note: Materials for the embellishments are listed separately.

- 7 large scraps of fancy fabrics for the block*

- 12″ × 12″ square of freezer paper for the block

- 12″ × 12″ square of muslin foundation fabric for the block

- 12″ × 12″ square of fusible knit interfacing for the block

- 18″ × 18″ square of muslin foundation for the quilt top

- 21″ × 21″ square of fabric for the quilt back

- 2 strips *each* 3″ × 11″ and 2 strips *each* 3″ × 15″ of lightweight silk for the inner border

- 2 yards of 2″-wide lace for the inner border

- 2 yards of ½″-wide rayon knitting ribbon for the inner border

- 2 yards of ½″-wide Lite Steam-A-Seam 2 for the inner border

- 2¼ yards of 1½″-wide wire-edged ribbon for the outer border

- 17″ × 17″ batting

- Embellishments: See Classic Crazy Quilt Stitches (page 36) and Three-Dimensional Flowers (page 43).

I recommend neutrals so the embellishments show up, but black is also great for a different look.

❋ Make the Block and Inner Border

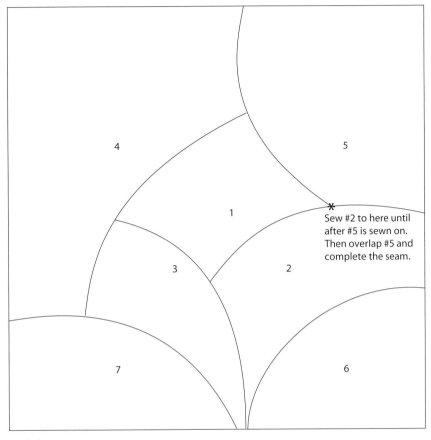

Block diagram

In the diagram: labels 4, 5, 1, 3, 2, 7, 6 mark the pieces. At the point marked with an asterisk:

*Sew #2 to here until after #5 is sewn on. Then overlap #5 and complete the seam.

I recommend using the freezer paper appliqué method (page 32) for constructing the block.

1. Using the block diagram (above) as a guide, make a 10″ × 10″ full-size finished block pattern. (Lines shown are the finished seamlines.) Trace this pattern onto a 12″ × 12″ muslin foundation and the freezer paper. When cutting the fabric pieces using the freezer-paper templates, remember to add seam allowances and to have extra fabric extend beyond the finished block perimeter line.

2. On the muslin foundation, piece your block, following the sequence on the block diagram. Interface the back with fusible knit interfacing. Mark a finished 10″ × 10″ perimeter line on the block. Machine zigzag stitch ¼″ outside the line and then trim the block to just outside the zigzag stitching to 11″ × 11″.

3. Center the block on the 18″ × 18″ muslin. Zigzag stitch it in place around the perimeter of the pieced block.

4. Sew each silk inner border strip with a ½″ seam allowance to the edges of the pieced block (the stitching line is the 10″ × 10″ perimeter line previously marked on the block). Flip and press each strip back over the bottom piece of muslin. Use a ruler to make sure your strips go on straight!

5. Pin lace over the silk border so that its edge is flush with the border/block seamlines. Fold miters at the corners of the lace as you pin it around the block, ending in a corner. Using clear thread, zigzag stitch along the pinned inner edge of the lace, all around the pieced block. You will embellish over this seam, so don't worry if the lace is not absolutely flush with the edge of the pieced block.

6. Zigzag over the lace miter fold in each of the 4 corners. Lift up the lace and trim the excess next to the stitching at each miter.

7. Press everything flat; then zigzag stitch around the lace's outside edge. Press again. You will have an extra margin of muslin and silk beyond the lace that will be covered last, so just leave it for now.

Your lace-bordered block is now ready to embellish.

Detail of spiderweb from *Floral Sampler* (full quilt on page 75)

❧ Add Embellishments

You'll embellish the borders and seams of the block with ribbon and thread embroidery first. You will then add the flowers and "critters." These embellishments include the lilac, dahlia, gathered ribbon flowers (variation 2), bellflower, rosebud, rickrack yarrow flower, ants, butterfly, spiderweb, and spider. See the instructions for making these embellishments (pages 43–57).

Embellishment diagram

Block embellishments

For the blocks, you'll need 6 kinds of white embroidery thread and 5 yards of 7mm variegated silk ribbon. I used a purple and maroon shaded ribbon.

1. Cover the mitered corner seams in the lace border with a line of cretan stitch in 6-ply floss. (I used rayon, but silk or cotton are also fine.)

2. Embroider the seams between the fancy fabric shapes in stitches of your choice using the different white threads. I used the fly, cretan, feather, chevron, and long and short chain stitches, with one type of stitch per seam. Because these stitches are in the background, they will be partially covered, so they do not need to be elaborate.

3. Use the 7mm silk ribbon in a loose herringbone stitch to cover the edge of the lace where it meets the block, forming a small inner border all around the block. Keep your stitching loose so the ribbon stays full.

Flowers

Refer to Eye Candy: Embellishment! (pages 36–57) for general instructions to create flowers using the materials listed for each. Place the flowers on the block according to the diagram.

Have fun with this! I've varied these flowers a bit from the ones in the general instructions. My dahlia in this version is made of detached chain stitches rather than silk ribbon stitches. And the bellflowers have been given raw-edged silk leaves that are held on with a central vein of chain stitching, instead of wire ribbon leaves.

Use your imagination to interpret these flowers in your own way!

Note: Amounts of materials needed are modest unless otherwise noted; a yard or so will do, plus a small number of the beads.

Lilacs (page 51)   Angelina fibers in white, blue, and mauve, with matching lightweight silk for backing the Angelina; fusible web; green embroidery floss; #11 green and yellow seed beads and beading thread; a small piece of green cotton felt

Dahlia (page 43)   2 colors of 3-ply wool tapestry yarn; yellow and green floss; a small circle of yellow fabric

Gathered ribbon flowers, variation 2 (page 46)   3 colors of ¼" Mokuba ombré picot ribbon; yellow floss; 7mm green silk ribbon twisted and straight stitched for the stems; fine sewing thread

Bellflowers (page 47)   Wire-edged ribbon in 1" and ½" widths; green wool tapestry yarn for the stems; 2mm green silk ribbon; green floss chain stitched on the leaves; green silk; fine sewing thread

Folded ribbon rosebuds (page 48)   1"-wide bias-cut silk ribbon; green tapestry yarn; fine sewing thread

Rickrack yarrow (page 50)   3mm rayon rickrack; green floss; fine sewing thread; beading thread

Critters

Ants (page 57)   Small nailhead beads; small bugle beads; #11 seed beads; black beading thread

Butterfly (page 56)   Hand-dyed silk; pink and orange floss; #8 Kreinik metallic fine braid thread; #11 seed beads

On the butterfly, use the buttonhole stitch to surround the wings. Complete the embroidery of the inner wings (see page 56). To make the body, sew 5 straight stitches the length you want the body to be. Then wrap the 5 threads with matching thread, around and around, up the length of the body. Add the eyes, antennae, and legs (see page 56).

Spider and spiderweb (page 56)   Silk sewing machine thread; 1 large bead for the body; 1 smaller bead for the middle; #11 seed beads; #15 seed beads; bugle beads; white beading thread

To make the spiderweb, take long straight stitches in silk sewing machine thread to form the long "spokes of the wheel." Couch them down with the same thread. The spokes are connected with a continuous spiral in more straight stitches that go around each spoke as it is reached. Some of these longer stitches can be couched as well.

Create your spider, the queen of this garden.

Vine

Fill in the gaps along the top edge and down the sides of the block, using a feather-stitched vine in 1-ply green wool tapestry yarn. Randomly add small 2-wrap French knots in 4mm silk ribbon along the vine.

Mitered corners and nice, finished ribbon edge

❀ Finish the Quilt

1. Iron the paper-backed ½"-wide Lite Steam-A-Seam 2 around the outside perimeter of the lace border, overlapping the lace by ¼". Remove the paper.

2. Beginning at a corner, place the ½" rayon knitting ribbon over the Lite Steam-A-Seam 2 and fuse into place, folding in the miters at the corners as with the lace (see page 91, Step 11).

3. Overlapping ¼" along the knitting ribbon, pin on the 1½" wire-edged ribbon for the final outer border, starting at a corner and folding in the miters as before. Either stitch it in place using clear thread in a machine zigzag, or appliqué it on by hand. Once the miters are sewn, trim off the extra fold of ribbon along the seam.

4. Trim the muslin foundation for the quilt top to ¼" inside the outer edge of the wire ribbon border.

5. Cut the batting to exactly the size of the finished quilt top (17" × 17"). (Mine ended up being 16½" × 17", I must confess.)

6. Cut the backing fabric so that it is 2" larger all around than the quilt top.

7. Place the quilt top facedown. Place the batting on top, and then place the backing fabric right side up. Fold the edges of the backing fabric around the edge of the batting and press. Pin this folded edge to the front of the quilt along the outside edges of the ribbon.

8. Whipstitch the layers together.

Waltie

Designed and made by the author, 2009.   Finished size: approximately 18″ × 18″

Waltie's picture was taken with a cell phone, so it's not very sharp. But when I saw it, I fell in love and just had to use it. That cat was a Dude!

This project has a pieced crazy quilt border surrounding a center that incorporates photo transfer and embroidery. The imagery was printed using iron-on inkjet transfer sheets (page 21) and was then ironed directly onto a vintage handkerchief. (I wish to thank Barbara Curiel for this fantastic concept; see her quilt *Little Flower* on page 62.) I used the hankie, which had a great diagonally striped printed border with flowers in the corners, as the basis for my embroidery … almost like a paint-by-numbers set.

Vintage hankies are good candidates for this technique because they have blank white center areas surrounded by highly embellishable frames. You can find inexpensive reproductions on eBay as well.

I pieced the borders and attached them to the hankie before beginning any of the embellishments. I like to work on pieces as a whole, but there is no reason you couldn't embellish each border strip before assembling the quilt.

The furry tan inner border was an irresistible addition at the last minute, which I appliquéd on after the quilt was assembled and embroidered. This inner border is optional, and the quilt is perfectly complete without it.

I kept to a pretty tight color scheme, using only browns and tans in the fabrics and green in the seam embroidery, with yellow-orange accents. Being this controlled certainly isn't mandatory, but it does serve to unify the piece.

Again, a piecing and embellishing diagram is given here, but obviously you will suit your own embellishments to the photo and handkerchief you choose to use.

WHAT YOU'LL NEED

For the center

These directions assume your hankie is 10½″ × 10½″. You may have to alter the lengths of your strips if you use a larger or smaller hankie.

- TAP (Transfer Artist Paper) or other T-shirt transfer paper (available at craft and quilting stores)

- Iron

- Vintage handkerchief with printed frame

- 10½″ × 10½″ square of muslin

- 10½″ × 10½″ square of fusible knit interfacing

- Embellishment supplies, such as beads, silk ribbon, various threads and flosses, and green felt for leaves

- Approximately ⅔ yard of trim to go around the hankie's printed image

- Water-soluble marker

For the borders

- Many small scraps of fancy fabrics for the outer borders

- 2 pieces *each* 6″ × 12″ of muslin and fusible knit interfacing for the side outer pieced borders

- 2 pieces *each* 20″ × 6″ of muslin and fusible knit interfacing for the top and bottom outer pieced borders

- 2 pieces 1½″ × 11″ and 2 pieces 1½″ × 13″ of furry fabric for the inner borders*

- Various embroidery threads

- Thick embroidery thread for couching around the furry inner border*

- Bugle and large seed beads for outlining the furry inner border*

- Rayon knitting ribbon

- Fabric glue

The inner fabric border is optional. If you wish, you can use trim or ribbon instead, or skip it.

For finishing

- 18″ × 18″ square of foamcore (available at craft stores)

- 17½″ × 17½″ square of fast2fuse interfacing or other stiff fusible interfacing (see Suppliers, page 127)

- 20″ × 20″ square of fabric for the backing

- 10″ piece of rat-tail cording to match the backing fabric

- 2 pieces 6″ × 18″ of muslin

- 2 pieces 30″ × 6″ of muslin

- 18″ × 18″ batting

- Beading thread for lacing

- Sewing thread to match the backing fabric

❇ Piece the Outer Borders

Use the curved-edge foundation piecing method (page 30) for all the outer pieced borders. Remember to include seam allowances and to extend your fabric shapes beyond the diagram's finished perimeter lines!

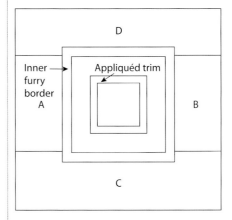

1. Using the border piecing diagrams as a guide, draw the block piecing diagrams onto the 4 muslin outer border strips. You can eyeball this by referring to the border diagrams.

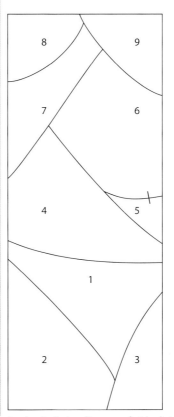

Border A piecing diagram—finished size 4″ × 10″

2. For border A, follow the piecing diagram. Join shapes 5 and 6 before you sew them to shape 4.

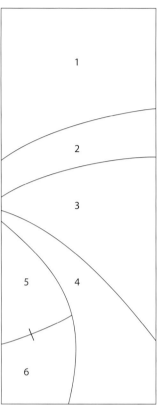

Border B piecing diagram—finished size 4″ × 10″

3. For border B, follow the piecing diagram. Again, join shapes 5 and 6 before you sew them to shape 4.

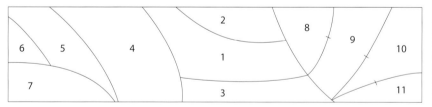

Border C piecing diagram—finished size 18″ × 4″

4. For border C, follow the piecing diagram, but this time join shapes 8, 9, 10, and 11 before sewing them to shape 1/2/3.

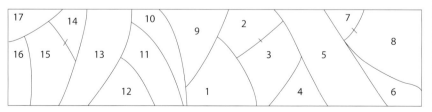

Border D piecing diagram—finished size 18″ × 4″

5. Although border D is more complex, it follows the same procedure. Follow the piecing diagram to join shapes 2 and 3 before sewing them to shape 1. Sew shapes 7 and 8 together before sewing them to shape 5/6, and sew shapes 14 and 15 together before sewing them to shape 13.

6. Use a water-soluble pen to mark the finished seamlines around the perimeter of the border sections at 4″ × 10″ for the sides (A and B) and 18″ × 4″ for the top and bottom (C and D). Interface each section with the fusible knit interfacing. Then zigzag stitch around the perimeter along the edges of the fancy fabrics to prevent fraying.

❀ Create the Center

How you embellish and trim the hankie, as well as the image you choose for the center, is up to you. I hope this project gives you some ideas to get started!

1. Choose the image and vintage hankie you wish to work with. Iron the hankie, and interface the back with the fusible knit interfacing.

2. My hankie had beautiful flowers framing the center. To add dimension, I wanted to have the flowers overlap the image. Using sharp-pointed embroidery scissors, I cut a slit following the outline of the flowers just in the areas that would overlap the printed image in the upper right and lower left corners. Use this technique on yours, or skip to Step 3.

3. Following the manufacturer's directions (and remembering to reverse your image), print your image onto the TAP or T-shirt transfer paper (see page 21).

4. Following the manufacturer's instructions, center the printed paper over the hankie, tucking the paper corners under the slits outlining the framing flowers. Iron the paper in an even circular motion. Peel up a corner to make sure the ink is transferring to the hankie. Peel off the paper when the transfer is complete, and allow the hankie to cool.

5. To add even more dimension, I cut slits along the outlines of the ears so they lie on top of the embellished frame. Be sure to keep them attached to Waltie's head! Use this technique on yours, or skip to Step 6.

6. Next, stitch the hankie to the 10½″ × 10½″ muslin square around its perimeter. Then, appliqué the trim around the perimeter of the transferred image, placing the ears on top of the trim.

Center with image and embroidery

7. Add embroidery to your piece. As you can see from the project photo, I added a combination of simple crazy quilt embroidery stitches and beads to make an intricate border around the central image. (For general embroidery information, see page 37.) The printed flowers on the hankie are embroidered with detached chain stitches in perle cotton. Over that I added 4mm silk ribbon in a ribbon stitch. All the flower centers were embellished with #11 seed beads. I added the rows of beaded leaves with fly stitch veins. I also added flower beads between the 4 corners of embellished flowers to strengthen the frame surrounding Waltie's face.

Though the transferred image can't take too much embroidery (it leaves holes), I was able to add Waltie's whiskers in long straight stitches, using silk sewing machine thread.

8. After embellishing, use the water-soluble marker to mark a 10″ × 10″ square around the perimeter of the center section to indicate the finished seamline.

❀ Assemble and Embroider the Quilt

1. Trim the A, B, C, and D border sections to ¾″ outside the marked perimeter line (the finished size of the section). Iron each section flat.

2. Make sure the finished sides of the center and the sides of the border are the same length. If they are not, adjust the length of the border to fit the center. Sew the side border sections (A and B) to the sides of the center. Trim all the seam allowances to ¼″. Press the seams *open* from the back to reduce bulk.

3. Attach the top and bottom border sections (C and D) as you did in Step 2. Again, press the seams *open* from the back.

4. Machine zigzag around the perimeter of the quilt. We don't want any fraying!

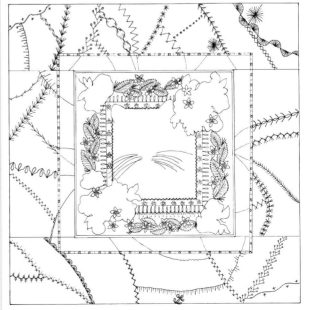
Stitch diagram

5. Now for the fun part of embroidering all the seams. I did not add any motifs inside the fancy fabric shapes, because I didn't want anything competing with the majestic Waltie! But feel free to add some if you desire. I've diagrammed the seam embroideries that I used; the types of threads are your decision.

6. If you wish to add the optional inner 1″ furry tan border, iron under ¼″ along the long edges of each strip of furry fabric (or the fabric or trim of your choice). Trim the length to fit and pin it into place, tucking under ¼″ on each end as well. Appliqué into place. I couched some narrow cording along the inside edge of this border and ran a line of bugle and small gold beads around the outside edge.

7. Add the name or other text. To write Waltie's name, I used narrow rayon knitting ribbon. I applied small dots of fabric glue to hold the ribbon in place in the shape of the cursive letters. Then I pressed it flat. I blanket stitched around all the letters with lightweight cotton Flower thread by DMC. Single or double strands of floss could work here, too. But the real secret is in using that glue!

❈ Finish the Quilt

I decided that the Waltie quilt needed to be tautly stretched so that his face would not appear wrinkled. Mounting the quilt onto foamcore and adding a finished back with a hanging cord was my method of choice.

To prepare the quilt for mounting on foamcore, sew the muslin strips to the borders of the quilt, short sides first and then top and bottom. The reason for the muslin strips is that they allow for shorter lacing stitches on the back, which iis much faster and easier than lacing with long stitches. Trim the corners to square up the quilt. Follow the instructions for How to Mount a Small Quilt Top onto Foamcore (page 87) to mount the quilt and finish it. When lacing a quilt top of this size, space the laces about ½″ apart and take a bite of about 1″ into the backing strips so they won't fray under the tension.

N is for Nora, 15″ × 15″, by the author, 2008

This quilt, which uses the same format as *Waltie*, was constructed in identical fashion. It is finished differently, however, with the "envelope method"—sewing a backing to the front, right sides together, and then turning that inside out.

There are always so many options in crazy quilting....

How to mount a small quilt top onto foamcore

You can use this method to mount any small work or block.

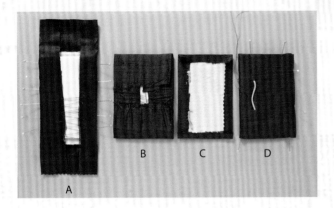

Foamcore can be purchased at any craft or framing store. It comes in large sheets, is acid free, and is not expensive. You can easily cut it to the size you need with a rotary cutter and ruler, or you can have it cut for you at the store. Here, my foamcore has been cut to the finished size of my 4″ × 6″ sample. In addition, I cut a piece of batting slightly larger. This batting will go between the foamcore and the quilt top.

Center the quilt top over the foamcore and batting, and fold the side edges to the back. Secure everything in place, using straight pins stuck directly through the layers into the edge of the foamcore. Begin lacing the side edges in place with a needle and a long, strong thread, removing the pins as you go. Start from the center and move to the edges to keep things square and the tension even (A). Keep checking to make sure your quilt is square as you do this.

Fold the top and bottom edges to the back and lace those as well, sewing through both layers where the fabric is folded at both ends. This adds a little extra bulk at the corners on the back; however, it is not a problem (B).

To create the backing, cut a piece of fast2fuse to the finished size of the quilt. The backing fabric is cut slightly larger than the fast2fuse, so there should be about ¾″ around the edges. Place the fabric wrong side up and center the fast2fuse on top. To create a nice finished edge, simply fold the fabric around the edge and onto the fusible side of the fast2fuse; press. (Note: I use some release paper to keep my iron from getting any glue on it.) Repeat this step with the remaining 3 sides of the back (C).

To make a hanger, measure and mark where you want the hanger to go on the backing piece. Use a very large needle and some pliers to pierce the back with some rat-tail cording. Secure the cording ends to the fast2fuse with several stitches, being careful not to sew through the backing fabric. Add your label to the back, if you like. Pin the back onto the foamcore, covering the lacing. Using strong sewing thread, whipstitch the back to the front along the edge (D).

Rejoice, 8½″ × 8½″, by the author, 2008

This little block looks nicely finished when mounted on foamcore.

"Sisters"

Crazy Quilt Scrapbook Page

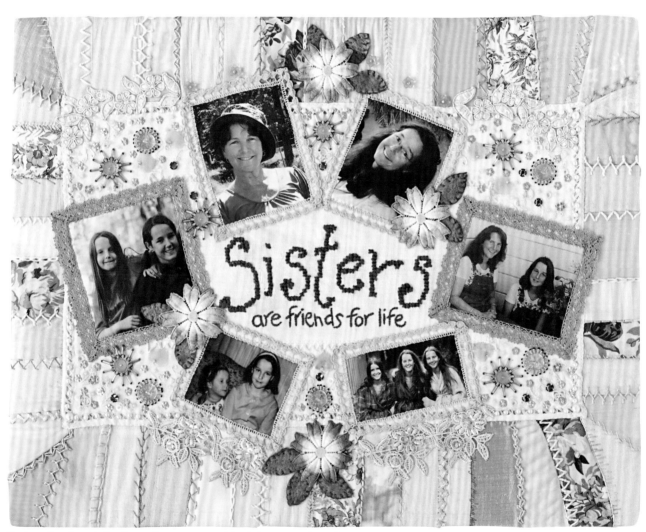

Designed and made by the author, 2009.   Finished size: approximately 20″ × 16″

My best friend and sister, Mary, turned 50 recently, so I decided to commemorate our lifelong friendship with a scrapbook-like crazy quilt. I used photos of us through the years (including one with our sister-in-law, Laura, who came into our lives more than 40 years ago and who is really the third sister). I added embellishments that I knew Mary would love. I also added a family memento.

What a great way to celebrate a relationship, event, or milestone!

The size of your own personal "scrapbook page" will be determined by the components you wish to include: How many photographs? How large will they be? What will you feature in the center of your "page"—a fancy handkerchief or something else? In my case, I used a cutwork lace placemat that belonged to our great grandmother.

Just think of the many possibilities for this center textile panel upon which you "mount" your photos! You could cut a section from an old and special dress or shirt, open up and use one of your husband's neckties, salvage a remnant from when you reupholstered your aunt's favorite chair, or piece together some old quilt blocks from your grandmother. You see? Almost any meaningful textile can be employed.

Begin by gathering your treasures, printing out your pictures (see page 20), and deciding on a color scheme. Grab some tracing paper, pull out your fancy fabrics, pick out some initial embellishment supplies, and prepare for a lot of fun. …

WHAT YOU'LL NEED

For the "scrapbook page"

- 22" × 18" piece of muslin for the foundation

- 20–25 small scraps of fancy fabrics

- 16" × 10" center panel of fabric, preferably a lovely or meaningful old textile

- Photos transferred onto fabric and backed with fusible knit interfacing (See page 20 for image transfer tips.)

- 12" × 8" size 10 piece of waste canvas for lettering

- 2 skeins of cotton floss

- Tracing paper

- Permanent marker

- Pencil

- 12" × 8" piece of background fabric for the lettering panel (I used old linen.)

- Water-soluble marker

- Temporary fabric adhesive spray (optional)

- Approximately 3½ yards of lace for photo frames

- Clear monofilament thread

For the embellishments

- Tracing paper and pencil

- 4 lace trim motifs (see Motifs, page 36)

- Painted lace flowers and needle-felted fabric or felt for the leaves

- Sequins

- #11 seed beads

- Buttons, bugle beads, pearls, flower, and leaf beads

- Beading needle and thread

- 10–15 different threads for seam treatments in the border

For finishing

- 2 strips 20½" × 6" of muslin

- 2 strips 6" × 27½" of muslin

- 20" × 16" piece of foam

- 20" × 16" piece of fast2fuse interfacing (see Suppliers, page 127)

- 21" × 17" piece of batting

- 22" × 18" piece of fabric for backing

- Strong thread for lacing (I used upholstery thread.)

- 10" of rat-tail cording

❧ Assemble Your "Scrapbook Page"

1. In the center of the 22" × 18" piece of muslin, mark an inner rectangle ½" smaller all around than your center textile panel.

2. Using the straight-edge foundation piecing method (page 27), sew shapes cut from fancy fabrics around the outside of the marked rectangle to form a frame. No measuring or preplanning allowed here! Just choose your fabrics, cut them, sew them, flip them, and press them—all the way around the perimeter of the muslin, angling the strips at the corners. (For ideas, refer to the project photo on page 88.) Be sure to place the pieces so they cover at least to the marked line from Step 1 and to the outside edges of the muslin.

3. Pin the center textile panel over this frame of strips. Zigzag machine stitch it in place with clear monofilament thread.

4. Arrange your photos the way you would like, but don't attach them yet. This step is to determine the placement and size of your phrase or word. After you've placed your photos, lay some tracing paper over the space where your word will go and write it, getting it just the way you want. Take the tracing paper to a table and retrace the letters with a thick black pen so you can see them well.

5. Place the waste canvas over the tracing paper. With a permanent marker, mark the waste canvas with your letters. (For more information about waste canvas, see Use Waste Canvas, page 17.)

Lettering on tracing paper is used to mark waste canvas.

6. Baste the waste canvas to the fabric on which you wish to embroider the letters. (I used some old linen. I did not want to stitch through the waste canvas directly onto my central textile panel because of the cutwork in it. But you could do so if you had a smooth surface to stitch on.) Using a simple cross-stitch in 12-ply cotton floss, cover the marked letters.

7. Remove the waste canvas with tweezers (see page 17).

8. Write any additional words below the cross-stitching with a water-soluble marker. Why not use your own handwriting? Embroider the additional words with the chain stitch in 2-ply cotton floss.

9. Iron under the edges of the letter-stitched fabric. Pin and sew it into place on the center panel, using clear thread in a zigzag stitch.

10. Iron under the edges of your transferred photos. Because I prefer not to pin my photos (which would leave holes), I spray the backs very lightly with temporary fabric adhesive and smooth the photos into position. If you do use pins, try to pin at the very edges of the photographs. Sew around their edges with clear thread in a narrow zigzag stitch.

11. Frame the photos with machine appliquéd lace, again using clear thread in a zigzag stitch to attach it. Start at a corner, leaving enough extra to form a miter. Fold miters in at the corners as you sew; you will tack those down by hand later, as well as the raw edges of the lace in the corner where you started. Trim off any extra when you've completed the frame.

Mitered lace corners

Now, put away that sewing machine!

❧ Embellish the Page

For this project, I used a lot of beads, buttons, and sequins to fill the areas in the center panel around the pictures, suggesting an inner frame. I also added some "pre-embellished" lace motifs, painted lace daisies, and buttonholed needle-felted embroidered felt leaves. (For more about beading and lace painting, see pages 39–41.) A line of pearls decorates the edge of my center panel.

1. Place tracing paper over your quilt and sketch where you want your main embellishment elements to go.

Your goal should be a balanced composition, though this does not mean it needs to be symmetrical.

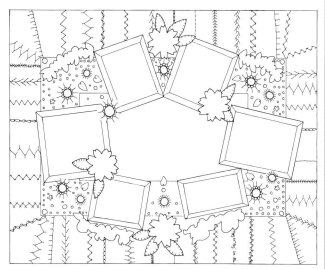

Here is a chart of my embellishments for this project. You may find it helpful to make your own chart.

2. Use a water-soluble marker to mark the embellishment placement on your "page," referring to your sketch as needed.

3. Sew on embellishments, starting with the largest ones first.

4. Embroider the seams of the fancy fabric outer borders. Vary the thicknesses and kinds of threads for textural interest, but keep the colors the same as your fabrics. You do not want to draw too much attention away from your photographs.

5. Use a damp, clean paper towel to remove any water-soluble ink that still might be showing.

6. With a water-soluble marker, mark a 20" × 16" finished-size rectangle on the quilt top.

❋ Finish the Quilt

As with *Waltie* (page 81), mounting this quilt over foamcore seemed the best way to finish it. I couldn't allow wrinkles to form in my sister's face, could I? She would have been mad at me if I had!

1. Trim the edges of the quilt top to ¾" larger than the marked finished size all around. Zigzag stitch around the quilt's perimeter. On the wrong side, mark a seamline with a ¼" seam allowance on one long edge of each of the 4 muslin strips.

2. Sew the shorter muslin strips to the top and bottom edges of the quilt top, aligning the seamlines with the marked 20" × 16" rectangle on the quilt top.

3. Repeat Step 2 to sew the remaining muslin strips to the side edges of the quilt top.

4. Follow the instructions in How to Mount Your Small Quilt Top onto Foamcore (page 87) to finish. For this project, I made the batting piece large enough to wrap to the back to give a nice smooth edge.

Tip

When lacing the back for this project, stitch 1" into the muslin and make your stitches ½" apart when lacing opposite edges. Remove the pins as you go. Sew through the folded-under layers at the corners of the side muslin strips.

The Beach

at Pilar, San Carlos, Mexico

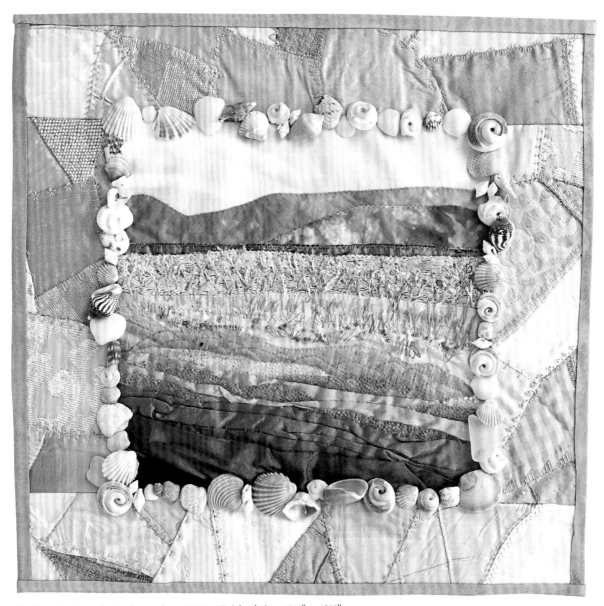

Designed and made by the author, 2009.   Finished size: 12½″ × 12½″

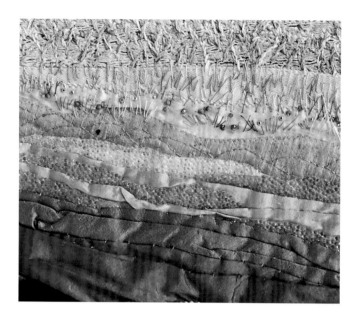

I spent many happy years as a "sane" quilter, making small landscapes out of cottons. Even though crazy quilting has taken over my life, I still like to make landscapes sometimes. But instead of cottons, I incorporate supplies from my crazy quilt stash and embellishment techniques I've learned since "going crazy."

The beach is a favorite subject of so many of us, and this project shows one way to enhance a seascape with different kinds of handwork, including sewn-on shells and beaded bubbles.

I always build a landscape from the background to the foreground, layering the fabrics on top of each other, as in collage. This helps give the illusion of depth. The sky, which goes on first, should be flat—I feel very strongly about this, because any texture or rumples in the fabric will bring it visually to the foreground, weakening the illusion of distance. So I always fuse my sky into place to make sure it stays flat. No stitched or quilted clouds for me (though I have seen some great trapunto clouds). Then I add mountains in the distance. In the middle ground, where sand meets terra firma, I add embellished details of plant life. The waves in the foreground go on last, with their bubbles.

Surrounding it all is an inner border of shells and beach glass from the beach at Pilar. And around that is a fused outer crazy quilt border that gives a great opportunity to use your sewing machine's fancy embroidery stitches.

WHAT YOU'LL NEED

For the seascape

- 10″ × 10″ square of muslin for the foundation
- Water-soluble marker
- 10″ × 4″ piece of fabric for the sky
- 10″ × 4″ piece of fusible web for the sky
- Scraps of fancy fabrics in tans, whites, and blues, with some light-toned, warm-colored cotton for the mountains
- Small scraps of white and blue silk for the waves (I used translucent silk habotai and chiffon.)
- Beads-2-Fuse beads (see Suppliers, page 127) *or* #11 clear seed beads for the bubbles in the waves
- Temporary fabric adhesive spray or pins
- Newsprint
- Size 75/11 sewing machine needle

For the embellishments

- 2 shades of #8 variegated perle cotton or silk in light gray
- 1 shade of #8 variegated perle cotton or silk in yellow
- 2 shades of light green floss
- Variegated machine quilting threads in green and yellow
- Tan sewing machine thread
- Sand-colored seed beads
- Beading thread and needle
- Seashells and beach glass (about 65 pieces)

For the borders, backing, batting, and binding

- 11″ × 13″ piece of muslin for the foundation
- Fancy fabrics in tans, whites, and light warm-colored scraps
- 12½″ × 12½″ square of backing fabric
- 12½″ × 12½″ square of lightweight batting
- Size 90 sewing machine needle
- Blue quilting thread
- ¼″-wide Lite Steam-A-Seam 2 fusible tape
- 4 strips ⅝″ × 12½″ of blue Ultrasuede for the binding

❧ Create the Seascape

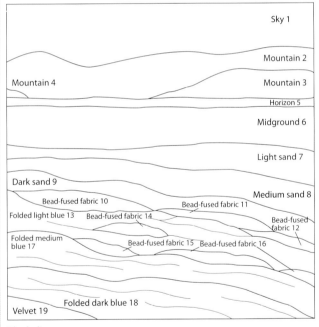

Block diagram

1. Using the block diagram as a guide, draw an 8″ × 8″ square finished pattern for the seascape block. The shapes in the pattern are finished sizes. Trace each shape onto tracing paper, adding a ½″ seam allowance to the *bottom* of each shape and 1″ to the perimeter edges, except for shapes 13, 17, and 18. These have an extra 2″ along their bottom edges (see page 96, Step 6).

2. Prepare the muslin by drawing an 8″ × 8″ square with the water-soluble marker. This is the finished size of the center section, so you will want your fabrics to extend beyond this perimeter line by at least 1″—it's better to have some extra margin than not enough!

3. Cut out the top piece (sky 1) from both the fabric and the fusible web. Fuse it into place at the top of the marked square on the muslin.

Tip

I fuse only the sky to the muslin, and I don't fuse the remaining elements because it is too hard to needle through fused fabric. I use temporary fabric adhesive to smooth my fabric shapes into place, and I complete the entire collage before going back and sewing all the edges by machine in a narrow zigzag with clear monofilament thread.

Place the fabric pieces wrong side up on newsprint and spray them lightly. Be sure your room is well ventilated. If you don't wish to use the spray, you can pin the fabrics into place.

4. Using the project photo (page 93) as a guide, build your collage on the muslin foundation, cutting out fabrics as you go and lightly spraying them with fabric adhesive before you smooth them into place. If you prefer to iron under the exposed top edges of your fabric shapes before spraying and smoothing them down, plan ahead and add a ½″ seam allowance. This is helpful when using fabrics that ravel easily.

Tip

Make sure that your horizon line, formed at the base of the mountains, is completely horizontal and straight. Use a ruler!

5. To create the bubbles where the waves meet the shore, I used a product called Beads-2-Fuse by the Warm Company (see Suppliers, page 127). Follow the manufacturer's directions to adhere this sticky fusible web to fabric; then dip it into a shallow dish of the beads (they have no holes). Lay a pressing cloth over the beads and apply a hot iron for 20 seconds to fuse them to the fabric. Once the beads are fused in place, you can cut through the fabric, spray the back with temporary adhesive, and apply it to your collage. Alternatively, you can use conventional beads and add the bubbles by hand after sewing all the waves into place.

6. For the water pieces, cut them oversized and iron under the exposed edge before spraying the temporary adhesive. Give the water in the foreground depth by scrunching up the fabric in horizontal wavelike lines as you apply it to your collage. Trim to fit after scrunching. Pin the waves in place. Tuck narrow strips of bubble fabric between some of the folds.

7. Before you begin sewing down the fabrics, change your sewing machine needle. That's right—you want a very sharp one that will leave the smallest hole possible, such as a Schmetz 75/11. Thread your machine with clear monofilament thread. Set the stitch to narrow, fairly close-together zigzag stitches. Put a few pins in the layers, just to secure them while you sew.

8. Sew down the layers from background to foreground, moving from the mountains down to the sand. However, no sewing machine would appreciate being asked to sew through the Beads-2-Fuse fabric, plus the waves look better hand appliquéd. Sew them down by hand, with the 3-D waves tacked into place with tiny invisible stitches. Use matching thread, as clear monofilament thread is horrible to sew with by hand.

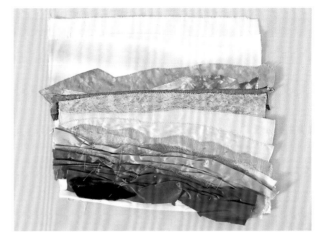

Seascape laid out and sewn down to water's edges

❧ Embellish the Seascape

Refer to the embroidery sampler and the tip on stitch resources (pages 36 and 37) for information on embellishing stitches.

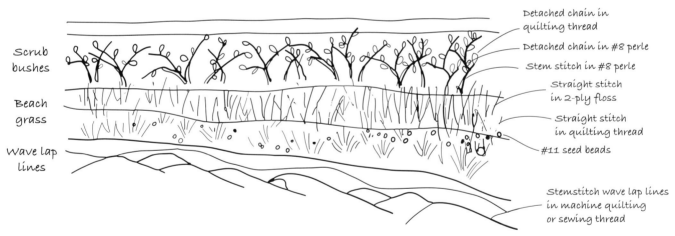

Embroidery diagram

Scrub bushes   #8 variegated perle cotton in 2 shades of light gray in a stem stitch; #8 variegated yellow silk perle in small detached chain stitches. Add detached chain stitches in single-strand variegated machine quilting thread.

Beach grass   Floss in 2 shades of green in long straight stitches. (The size of the stitches gets smaller toward the left side of the seascape to suggest perspective.) Fill in with more straight stitches in variegated machine quilting thread. Add a sprinkling of seed beads, as shown at the base of the sea grass along the sand.

Wave "lap lines"   Sand-colored thread in a stemstitch

With a water-soluble marker, measure and mark an 8″ × 8″ square on your block. Trim the block to 8½″ × 8½″. Machine zigzag stitch around the perimeter.

❧ Make the Crazy Pieced Outer Border

Because all the fancy fabrics are similar in tone and value, their placement can be random and spontaneous. Now is your chance to use all those tiny bits you've been saving!

The borders will be only 2″ wide finished. Rather than make each narrow strip individually, fuse fabrics onto an 11″ × 13″ piece of foundation fabric and embroider the seams by machine. From this, cut the individual border strips. This is a real time-saver, and it looks great! To piece the border, use the fused appliqué method (page 33), but this time, when cutting out the pieces, add a ¼″ seam allowance and iron under the scrap edges before applying the fusible tape.

Diagram of border before it is cut into strips 2½″ wide

1. Iron under a scant ¼″ along one edge of each scrap of fancy fabric before fusing it onto the muslin. Attach a piece of ¼″ Lite Steam-A-Seam 2 fusible tape to the folded-under edge; fuse the scrap into place, overlapping the previous scrap's raw edge. Add scraps from the top of the muslin on down, so there are no raw edges exposed as you go. (Note: Some scraps will need more than one edge folded under.)

2. When the entire piece of muslin is covered, press everything flat. Now you're ready to do decorative machine embroidery along the seams.

Tip

Before you begin embroidering, try out your stitches on a sample scrap. Use a size 90 needle in your sewing machine. To simplify the project and unify the look of the border, I recommend using the same thread for all the seams. (You can change threads, but as a design element, I don't think it is necessary.) I used quilting thread because it is a little heavier than regular thread, so the stitches show up better. Stitch slowly, so that your machine won't skip any stitches. But if it does skip a little, just keep going. It doesn't matter!

3. When all the seams are embroidered, press the entire piece flat from the back.

4. With a rotary cutter and ruler, measure and cut 4 border strips 2½″ wide. (Don't they look great?) Immediately zigzag the edges of the strips.

5. Decide which border strips you want for the sides and attach them to the block, using a ¼″ seam allowance. Then trim them to length and press *open* the seams to reduce bulk. Sew on the top and bottom strips, trimming them to size after they are sewn on, and press open the seams. Zigzag the raw edges of the trimmed border pieces.

How to prepare shells for embellishment

Here is an easy way to turn shells into embellishments without drilling holes in them: Essentially you glue a threaded button onto the back of the shell. The threads are pulled to the back of the block and knotted securely into place. I used to use small buttons for this, but they are hard to find and expensive. Now I make my own "buttons," and it couldn't be easier. You can use this method to sew on various small treasures for any project.

WHAT YOU'LL NEED

- Top from a plastic food container, with rim cut off
- 1 large needle and 1 medium needle
- Paper hole puncher
- Strong beading thread
- E-6000 glue (available at craft stores)
- Toothpick
- Newsprint
- Small shells and beach glass

1. To make the first button, use the large needle to poke 2 little holes near the edge of the plastic lid, $\frac{1}{16}''$ apart.

2. Center the paper hole puncher over the holes and punch out the button.

3. Thread the button with a 12″ strand of beading thread, leaving 2 tails 6″ long. Repeat Steps 1 and 2 to make as many threaded buttons as you need.

4. With a toothpick, spread a small amount of glue over the threaded side of a button.

5. Push the button onto the back of a shell so there is complete surface contact between button and shell. (For a larger shell, use 2 buttons.) Don't forget the beach glass— you can glue threaded buttons to it, too!

6. Place the glued shells on newsprint, with the threads hanging free. Allow to dry for 24 hours.

7. To sew the shells and glass onto a project, simply thread the tails *through the smaller needle*, one at a time, and bring them to the back of the block. Tie the threads in a triple knot; then thread both tails into a needle. Make a small stitch and tie off the threads again. Your shell should be very securely attached.

❀ Attach the Shell Inner Border

Detail of shell border

After you've prepared your shells, simply sew them on one at a time until the border is filled in. Start with the largest elements in the corners and centers of the borders, and then gradually add the rest. To fill in some gaps, I did use a few tiny commercially drilled shells, which are sold cheaply on strings in bead stores and at tourist souvenir shops.

❀ Add the Ultrasuede Binding

1. Lay out your backing fabric, wrong side up, then the batting, and then the quilt top right side up. Using a ruler, make sure all 4 corners are perfectly square; trim through all layers with a rotary cutter to square up if necessary.

2. Pin the layers together around the perimeter and machine zigzag through all layers around the edge, removing the pins as you go.

3. Press ¼" Lite Steam-A-Seam 2 tape along all 4 outer edges of the quilt, on the front and back.

4. Starting on the front, on the left side, peel off the Lite Steam-A-Seam 2 paper backing. Align an edge of a strip of Ultrasuede along the Lite Steam-A-Seam 2, just covering it. Press it into place with your fingers (the tape is sticky), and then carefully fuse it in place with an iron.

5. Flip the quilt over. Remove the paper backing on the same quilt edge. Fold the Ultrasuede to the back of the quilt and fuse it into place with an iron.

6. Repeat Steps 4 and 5 for the right side of the quilt.

7. Before fusing the top edge's binding, tear off enough Lite Steam-A-Seam 2 tape to cover the ends of the Ultrasuede that is already fused on at the quilt's corners; finger-press it in place. Do this at all 4 corners on the front and the back of the quilt.

8. Remove the paper backing along the quilt's top front edge. Fuse the Ultrasuede along this front edge, fold it to the back, remove the paper backing, and fuse the Ultrasuede in place. Repeat for the quilt's bottom edge.

Crazy Quilt Soft Doll

The Dreaming Maiden

Designed and made by the author, 2009.   Finished height: approximately 10″

This flat little doll provides a good opportunity to try out some piecing and embellishment ideas. Her face and clothing come alive with the addition of embroidery and fancy trims. The bouquet hides her hands, her skirt covers her feet, and her hair hides her ears, so we don't need to worry about those sometimes difficult-to-portray details. The components are prepared separately and then fitted together, so the construction is a little bit unusual. Just take it slowly, and you'll be fine. And have fun dressing her!

WHAT YOU'LL NEED

- Tracing paper and pencil
- ¼ yard of muslin for the foundation pieces
- 5″ × 8″ piece of flesh-toned fabric for the face and neck
- Chalk pencils in white and blush (*optional*)
- Machine sewing thread in colors for face: brown, 2 shades of blue, and red
- ½ yard of lightweight fusible knit interfacing
- Several different kinds of fibers in the hair color of your choice
- Clear monofilament thread
- Variety of fancy fabric scraps for the skirt and bodice
- White fabric scrap for the sleeves
- Embellishment threads, trims, and beads
- Water-soluble marker
- Quilt batting scraps for the face, bust, sleeves, and stuffing the doll
- 8″ × 12″ piece of fabric for backing the doll

❈ Trace and Prepare the Foundation Pieces

1. Trace the doll patterns (page 108) onto tracing paper. Be sure to trace the facial features, or draw your own if you prefer. If you'd like to change the size of the doll, you can reduce or enlarge the templates on a copy machine. These templates are shown in finished size. *Be sure to mark the seamline and add a ½″ seam allowance to the template pieces when you trace them.*

2. With the water-soluble marker, transfer your pattern components to individual pieces of muslin. (Use a lightbox, a glass-topped table, or a window.) The muslin pieces will be the foundations for the doll components that you will piece and embellish before assembly. Be sure to mark the seamline and add seam allowances on each piece.

Tip

It would be prudent to prepare a couple of extra muslin and flesh-toned squares for the face/neck piece, as you may not get the face just right on your first try. It took me a couple of tries!

3. You may choose to create your own piecing diagram for the bodice and skirt. If you use mine, follow the diagram on page 104 as a guide to draw the piecing diagram onto the muslin pieces.

At this point you will have six patterns traced onto muslin, ready for embellishment: the face/neck, hair, bodice, skirt, and two arms.

Muslin foundation pattern pieces, with both seam allowances and seamlines marked and face drawn

❁ Make the Face and Neck

The main hair piece (no pun intended) will actually be used as the background for the face, arms, and bodice.

1. Cut out a 4" × 5" rectangle of flesh-toned fabric for the face/neck. Baste it to the face/neck muslin piece. The face design on the muslin will show through the skin fabric, so you don't have to mark the face.

2. Embroider the facial features by hand, using a fine stem stitch and straight stitches for the nose (see page 37). I used machine sewing thread and a fine needle for this embroidery. Use very small, fine stitches (smaller than ¹⁄₁₆"), because the facial features are so tiny. This might take a couple of attempts; faces can be very tricky. Just go slowly and be patient, making another one if you need to.

3. After the face is embroidered, use a white chalk pencil to very carefully color in the whites of the doll's eyes. A faint amount of blush could be added to her cheeks with a chalk pencil as well. But please, use a very light touch!

❁ Make the Hair

1. Fuse lightweight fusible knit interfacing to the back of the hair muslin pattern piece. Using clear thread in a zigzag stitch, machine couch several kinds of threads and yarns in place, side by side, on both sides of the piece.

2. On the face/neck piece, couch threads for bangs; then add a few strands along either side of the head, defining the shape of the face and neck to below where the bodice will be attached.

Hair foundation piece and face/neck piece, with hair fibers couched on

3. On the face/neck, trim the fabric layers to ½" around the edges of the hair. Fold under the fabric layer edges all the way around the head, so that only the face and hair show. Nicely round the top of the head—some of the yarn ends will be folded under in this area.

4. Pin the face/neck on top of the couched hair piece. The hair should blend nicely between the 2 pieces. Add more hair strands, if needed, to help blend the layers.

5. Cut out a small oval shape of batting, slightly smaller than the face. Poke it in behind the face with the tips of small scissors to make the face come forward a little. Appliqué the face/neck to the hair, using a strong thread, such as beading thread. Your stitches will disappear in the couched yarns.

❋ Make the Sleeves, Skirt, and Bodice

Piecing diagram

1. Cut out the white sleeve fabric, place it over the muslin arm patterns, and zigzag stitch (using a narrow stitch) just outside the seamlines. Trim close to the zigzag stitches and set aside.

2. Using the crazy piecing method of your choice, cover the muslin skirt and bodice pieces with your selection of fancy fabrics. I used Curved-Edge Foundation Piecing (page 30).

3. Fuse some lightweight fusible knit interfacing to the back of the skirt and bodice pieces (and to the sleeves if you choose to embroider them).

4. Machine zigzag stitch just outside the seamlines for each pieced component to prevent fraying. You will trim to the zigzag stitching when it is time to assemble the doll.

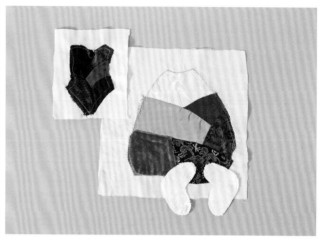

Pieced doll components, ready for embellishment

5. Embellish according to your own whim! In my example, I used some trims as the bases of my seam treatments, attaching them by machine with clear thread. (Trim is an excellent way to achieve lots of interest and detail without having to do much stitching.) The embroidery on the bodice had to be fine because the scale is so small, so I used machine sewing thread for some of it.

Tip

Keep in mind that the sleeves will cover the lower part of the bodice and the top of the skirt, so you do not need to overembellish these areas. Also, the bouquet covers most of patch 1 of the skirt, so there is no need to add any embellishments to that area.

Detail of bodice embellishment

Detail of skirt embellishment. Note the use of multiple trims along a single seamline.

❀ Assemble the Components

1. Trim any excess fabric up to the zigzagged stitching along the bodice seamlines. Pin some tiny lace edging where the bodice neckline will be, if you desire. A necklace of small pearl beads may be attached to either side of the neck.

2. Appliqué the bodice neckline and shoulders in place over the face/neck/hair assembly. Starting in the center neckline, work to the outside end of one shoulder and then go back to the center and appliqué to the outside end of the other shoulder. Stop. Leave the bodice sides open until after you've attached the top of the skirt beneath the bodice. This will help you align the skirt before you sew everything together.

3. Trim any extra fabric off the skirt next to the zigzagged stitching at the seamlines. Slip the top of the skirt under the bottom edge of the bodice, lining up the center bottom of the bodice with the top center of the skirt. These pieces overlap. Pin in place and appliqué together, again working from the center out to one hip and again from the center to the opposite hip.

4. Turn under the top of the sides of the skirt and the sides of the bodice on either side of the figure. Hand appliqué the pieces into place onto the hair. I use the needle-turn appliqué method (turning under the seam allowance with your needle as you sew). Now is your chance to give your doll a cute little waist, depending on how much of the bodice you fold inward!

At this point, you have the bodice and skirt centered and sewn to the background face/hair assembly.

Tip

If you want your doll to have a maidenly bosom, make a tiny tube of batting. Before appliquéing, use a pair of scissors to poke it into place beneath the bodice.

5. Clip the sleeves ¼″ into the seam allowances at the inner elbows. Line up the tops of the sleeves flush with the bodice shoulders. You may find you prefer the sleeves narrower than they are given in the pattern. If so, just fold them in a little more. Fold under the sleeves along the inside arm edge and at the shoulder. Pin this onto the bodice and hair and appliqué into place.

6. Fold under the outside edge of the forearm at the wrists out to the elbow. Pin and appliqué, leaving ⅛″ free at the outer edge past the hair seamline. Leave the ends of the arms open at the wrists. (Because our doll is holding a big bouquet of flowers, there are no hands to construct, and the ends of the arms need not be appliquéd.)

7. The bouquet in my example is created from machine embroidered flowers cut from some embroidered chiffon, as well as from snipped pieces of embroidered trim, all appliquéd on. You could also create your own flowers from silk ribbon, sew on floral beads, or try any other option you choose. Sew them on one by one until you have a pleasing arrangement.

Doll bouquet

8. A few of these premade flowers are sewn into the hair along the groove formed where the head is sewn onto the hair piece.

At this point, the face, bodice, skirt, and sleeve pieces are all applied to the hair foundation piece. Now your doll is ready to finish into its final form.

Finish Your Doll

1. Cut away any excess fabric from the perimeter of the doll, leaving ½″ of the muslin foundation fabrics.

2. To give dimension to the arms, roll up 2 batting scraps 2″ × 2″ and insert 1 into each arm from the open side.

3. To create the template for the doll back, with the front of the doll facing up, trace around the doll onto tracing paper, including the ½″ seam allowance all around. Everyone's doll will be slightly different; that is why I am having you trace your own back template.

4. Place the doll back template right side up on the *wrong* side of the backing fabric; trace and cut out.

5. Cut out 2 layers of batting for the doll's stuffing, using your back template as a pattern. Trim off about ¼″ all the way around. (You don't want extra batting in the seam.) Baste the batting to the inside of the backing fabric to prevent shifting. These stitches will be removed later.

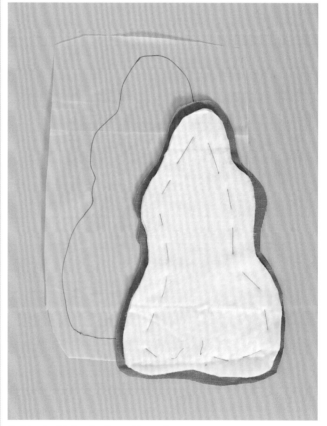
Doll back with batting basted into place

6. Sew the doll together by hand, because you will have much more control that way than if you do this by machine. Fold in the edges of both the front and back pieces and pin them together as you go. Take your time here and use lots of pins. You may need to trim the batting as you pin or clip areas where there are angles (such as at the elbows) before you fold in the seam allowances.

7. Whipstitch together the folded-under edges all the way around the doll, removing pins as you go.

Your Dreaming Maiden is now finished … and ready to be filled with new dreams!

Susan Elliott made her own incredible interpretation of this project, following the pattern and instructions but tweaking them to suit her own vision (see *Your Majesty*, at right). Isn't she regal? Susan says about her doll: "The queen you see here is not meant to be a version of any one queen in particular, though her overall appearance is most accurately a British monarch. Her hair is inspired by Mary, Queen of Scots; her face is Queen Maud of Norway; her veil (which functions as the hairpiece) is borrowed from the Bolshevik queens; her dress is inspired by the coronation gown of Queen Elizabeth II; and her jeweled orders and ribbon sash are all British. The skirt was a joy to research and stitch. The dress is modeled after the gown worn by Queen Elizabeth for her coronation in 1953. It includes motifs from Great Britain, as well as from other members of the British Commonwealth. You might recognize the Scottish thistle, the Canadian maple leaf, the New Zealand fern, and the Welsh leek, in addition to the Tudor Rose."

Your Majesty, 9″ × 15″, by Susan Elliott, 2009

In every woman there is a Queen.
Speak to the Queen and the Queen will answer.
—Norwegian Proverb

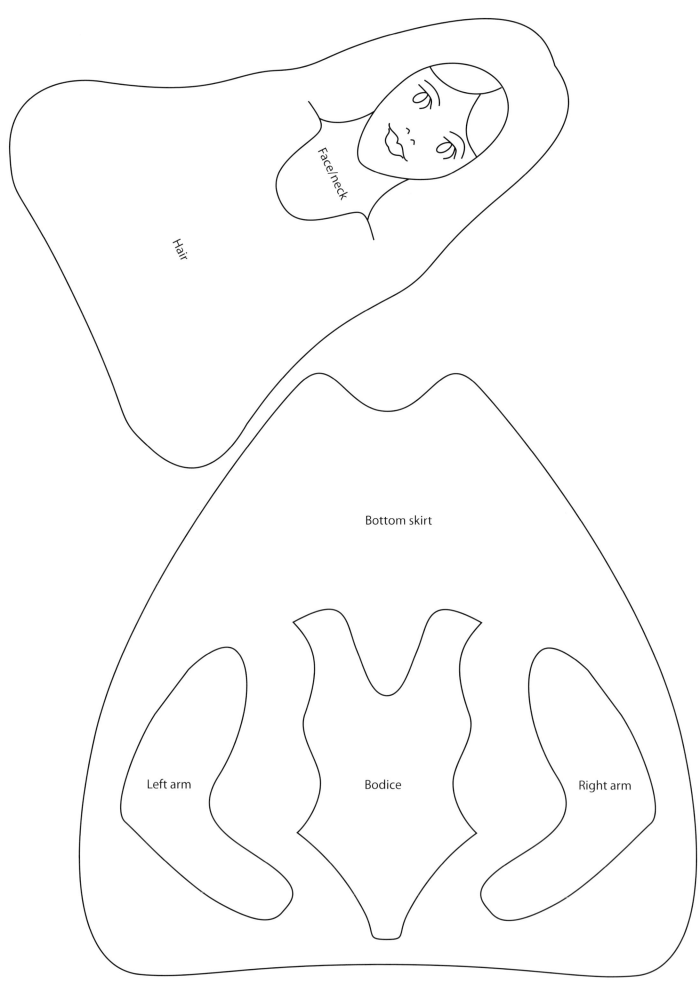

Face/neck

Hair

Bottom skirt

Left arm

Bodice

Right arm

Work in Progress:

A Crazy Quilt from Start to Finish

Crazy Happy Flowers, 40″ × 40″, designed and made by the author, 2009

In this chapter, I invite you to make your own wholecloth crazy quilt. As I made this quilt, I took a series of in-progress photographs—mostly of the quilt on the design wall—so I could share with you here, step by step, what went into my thinking and the making of this project. You'll see how it all comes together, from the initial piecing to the final binding.

I also hope to demonstrate that you don't have to spend months and months making a crazy quilt. In this quilt, the stitching is simple, bold, and graphic along the seams; there are no motifs within the patches (as are so often included in traditional crazy quilts); the medallion and fans have a base of floral raw-edge machine appliqué beneath the hand embellishments; and much interest and detail were introduced by the simple addition of some fancy lace. All these elements are time-savers. You won't make this in a week, or maybe even in a month … but as far as crazy quilts go, this one is quick!

I've included many technical tips to help you achieve a quilt that behaves—one that hangs or lies flat, with embellishments that are well supported and that will never sag, all nicely squared up. This quilt has a false back and basted batting inside to help stabilize it; over that, it has a dressy back for show.

As with all the projects in this book, consider the following directions as a formula only. You can change any of the variables to suit your own taste. Perhaps you want a smaller version or different colors in the background. (For my quilt, I chose to use only shades and hues of one color—blue.) Perhaps you want to use something besides silk ribbon in the seam treatments, or you would rather create a landscape for the medallion instead of a floral collage. As always, it is up to you.

WHAT YOU'LL NEED

- 4⅛ yards of 44"-wide muslin for the foundation, false back, medallion background, and quilted backings for the medallion and fans

- Variety of floral cotton fabrics for the appliqué*

- Large variety of fancy blue fabrics for the background piecing (Scraps are fine.)

- 1 yard of fine white fabric for the white rings (I used a cotton/silk blend.)

- ¾ yard of fabric for the background of the corner fans (I used a pink abstract floral fabric.)

- 1½ yards of 24"-wide fusible knit interfacing

- 4 yards of 2½"-wide lace as a border for the center medallion and fans (I used Mokuba #61096K.)

- 1½ yards of 42"-wide tightly woven fabric for the dressy back

- 44" × 44" piece of batting or cotton drapery lining fabric to use as batting

- 5 yards of 1½"-wide wire-edged ribbon for the binding

- 5 yards of rickrack for the binding's inner edge

- 1 yard each of wire-edged ribbon in several colors and widths for the flowers

- 25 yards of 13mm silk ribbon for the herringbone borders

- Size 18 chenille needle

- Many colors of 4mm and 7mm silk ribbon for the flowers and seam stitching

- Beads, buttons, charms, threads, and other embellishments of your choice

- Several kinds of sequins for embellishing the lace and #11 seed beads to secure them

- #11 beading needles

- Beading thread

- Machine quilting thread for the white rings (I used Sulky Sliver metallic thread)

- Small sharp scissors

- 25 buttons for the back

- Clear monofilament thread

- Temporary fabric adhesive spray

- Newsprint

*¼ yard pieces are enough for all but the largest flowers; for those, get ¾ yard, so you can fussy cut the large blooms.

Tip

I always use the design wall when I am creating my crazy quilts, every step of the way. It is important to me to view each quilt as a composition, not just as a random assortment of fabrics, which most of the traditional crazy quilts were. The design wall keeps the whole picture in front of me as my quilt develops. To make a simple design wall, refer to page 18.

How to measure large circles of any size

Create your own very simple compass

Tie a marking pen to a piece of string. Measure the string to the length of half your intended circle's diameter (the radius). Mark this distance with a pen. Pin the string on that mark to your fabric. Holding down the pin, pull the string until it is taut; then draw your circle, keeping the pen perpendicular to the fabric and sweeping around from the center. This will give you the basic shape. Use this method to mark an 18″ circle for your medallion, or create a template using the following method. (Or maybe you have a circle ruler or a nice clean pizza pan to trace.)

Create your own template

1. Cut out a square of thin paper (the yellow quilt design tracing paper that comes on a roll is perfect for this, but you could use cheap wrapping paper too), slightly larger than the finished circle will be.

2. Fold this paper in half diagonally and then into quarters. Crease the paper sharply. Measure 8¼″ (or the radius of the circle) along each side of the folded triangle and mark the paper. Match the 2 marks as you fold and crease the paper into eighths. Measure and mark 8¼″ along the unmarked edge of the triangle, match the marks, fold, and crease. Repeat this for a total of 6 folds, so that your tracing paper is divided into 64ths.

3. Measure 8¼″ one last time on the unmarked edge and cut through all the layers between the marks. Unfold the tracing paper to get a circle 16½″ in diameter.

4. Iron out the creases in the paper. It is now ready to be used to mark the medallion foundation fabric or to be cut in fourths as a fan pattern.

✿ Make the Medallion and Fans

Here you will create machine-appliquéd collages from floral fabrics for the medallion and fans. These will then be appliquéd onto another layer of fabric, which will become the white ring borders.

Create the appliqué

1. Fussy cut lots of flowers from your printed fabrics. No margin is needed around them. I used many different fabrics and sizes of flowers. A pair of small sharp scissors is useful here. Why not invest in a new pair, just for this?

Some of the flower fabrics used in the collages

2. For the medallion, measure and mark a circle 18″ in diameter on the muslin or on a background fabric of your choice. (See How to Measure Large Circles of Any Size, at left.) This full circle will be the foundation piece for the center medallion flower collage. Cut it out on the line.

3. For the fans, make a template as described in How to Measure Large Circles of Any Size (at left) for a circle 16½″ in diameter. Fold the circle into quarters, press, and cut along the folds to create 4 fans. Trace these patterns onto muslin or other background fabric and cut them out. Press under ¼″ along the curves.

4. Lay out the medallion and fan backgrounds on a work surface where you can keep your fabric collage undisturbed as you build it. Keep an iron handy to ensure that the cut-out flowers lie flat.

Tip

I use a temporary fabric adhesive spray to smooth my floral elements into place while I work. No pinning or fusing is necessary. But you should be in a well-ventilated room when you use the spray.

5. It is best to begin making the medallion and fan collages by arranging your largest flowers first. Place a flower face-down on some newsprint and give it a very quick, light spray. Then simply smooth the flower into place, spray side down, onto the foundation fabric.

Here, I began building the flower collage.

6. As you compose your collages, it is quite easy to lift up flowers already in place to tuck one flower under the edge of another. Be sure that any darker-colored flowers don't show through lighter ones on top of them. If they do, lift up the lighter one and trim the darker one to just below where the light one overlaps it.

7. When you are finished and happy with your designs, press them flat.

Detail of one of my collages, ready to be sewn down

8. Begin sewing down the flowers in the center of the medallion or fans. I use a clear monofilament thread in my machine, with a thin embroidery or lingerie thread in the bobbin. The zigzag stitch is set at 2mm wide and 1.5mm long. (This is actually a modern version of Broderie Perse!) Stitch around all exposed edges of all flowers.

Tip

You could use machine embroidery thread in various colors as a design element if you choose, when sewing down your collage. I prefer the see-through thread for two reasons: I don't have to keep changing threads on my machine, and if my stitching gets a little irregular, it won't show.

9. Press the medallion and fans flat when stitching is complete and clip off any loose threads.

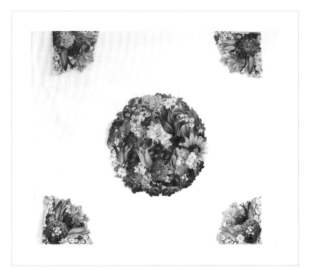

Medallion and fans on the design wall. Note that I have purposely left flowers and leaves hanging over the edge of my foundation fabric.

Frame the medallions and fans

The medallion and fans will be machine appliquéd onto another layer of fabric—the one that will form the white rings around them.

MEDALLION

Cut a 22″ × 22″ square from the white ring fabric. Using temporary fabric adhesive, spray the back of the appliquéd medallion and center it over this square. Pin and machine appliqué the medallion around its perimeter edge onto the white ring fabric, using the same thread and zigzag stitch as you used when sewing down the flowers. Clip off any threads hanging loose on the back. You will trim the square into a circle shape later.

Tip

At this stage I recommend preparing the medallion for embellishment by interfacing the back with knit fusible interfacing and zigzagging around the perimeter of the square.

FANS

Cut 4 squares 11″ × 11″ from the white ring fabric. Spray and place each fan on its square, with the corners lined up. Pin and machine appliqué the turned-under curved edge of the fan, as well as the raw-edge overhanging leaf and flower shapes, with the same thread and zigzag stitch as used for the flowers.

As with the medallion, I recommend that you interface the back of the squares and zigzag stitch around their perimeters. The curved shape of the white rings will be cut later.

Add embellishments

Embellishments I added in the center medallion

Adding the three-dimensional flowers on top of the appliquéd collages is a lot of fun. I chose to create wired ribbon bells, wired ribbon leaves, two kinds of ombré ribbon circles (of the gathered ribbon flower, variation 2, page 46), rickrack yarrow flowers, folded rosebuds (variation 1), gathered ribbon flowers in 13mm silk ribbon, and one central flower comprised of cotton petals with a center cut out of some old needle-punch work I had on hand. I sewed on some individual Turkish oya needlework flowers and made some small detached chain-stitch daisies.

Instructions for creating all of these flowers (except the oya and the needle-punch work) can be found in Three-Dimensional Flowers (pages 43–55). To view more oya flowers or to learn more about this wonderful Turkish needle lace, search "oya lace" on the Internet; to purchase some, see Suppliers (page 127).

I also appliquéd some lace leaves and little daisy trim flowers. Finally, I couldn't resist sewing on some brass stamped bees. If something among your treasures looks like a good fit to you, add it!

I will bead the centers of many of these flowers in a later step in the construction process.

This large brass bee is attached by stitches around the base of each leg.

🌼 Piece the Wholecloth Crazy Background

Cut a piece of muslin 44″ × 44″. This will be your foundation for the wholecloth piecing. The finished quilt will be 40″ × 40″; the extra muslin is a helpful margin while piecing. Mark this 40″ × 40″ square *very carefully*.

The medallion and fans will be placed in the center and the corners and will be appliquéd over this background piecing after it is completed.

In this project, I used a combination of the methods described in Four Ways to Build a Crazy Quilt Block (pages 26–35). Sometimes I use machine appliqué, sometimes I piece chunks before appliquéing the unit as one piece, and sometimes I foundation piece directly onto the wholecloth foundation, using both straight and curved seams. I even fused a few awkward-sized patches in there. This is crazy play at its most fun!

In crazy quilts, we are putting together a puzzle, and there are different ways to make the pieces fit, depending on the situation. You do *not* have to plan your piecing ahead of time; instead, you can build your crazy patch area as you go. Really, you can!

Before you begin: Some piecing tips

- Before you commit to cutting your precious fabric, you can audition the shape with tracing paper. Lay the paper over your pieced surface and draw where the next piece will fit into the puzzle. *Refine which shape you want and use the paper shape as a template to cut your fabric.*

- When you want to use a lightweight fabric that is too translucent, simply cut a second piece of fabric in the same shape to back it. Treat the two pieces as one when you sew them into place. You can also overlay a piece of lace fabric onto a solid fabric and treat that as one piece of fabric.

Top to bottom: Translucent silk; the same silk laid over cotton; and lace laid over cotton

- When you topstitch appliqué a piece of fabric in which two sides have turned-under edges that create a corner, it is much better to first sew from the corner and down one side, then from the corner and down the other side, rather than around in one continuous seam. There is less chance for distortion this way.

- When you get to the perimeter edge of a pieced block or quilt, machine baste the outer edges onto foundation fabric to prevent "floppage."

- If you find, when appliquéing a piece or chunk in place, that you have not quite covered the edge of the neighboring piece, fear not. Just go back and zigzag stitch over that exposed raw edge. Remember, this seam area is going to be covered by glorious embroidery, so there is room for a little error. One of the best things about crazy quilting is how forgiving it is.

- Do interface those silk velvet scraps before you piece them. You'll be so glad you did.

Start at the center circle

1. Measure and mark a circle 20″ in diameter in the center of the muslin (see page 112). In the corners, measure and mark fans with 10″-long straight sides. You will be piecing just beyond these marks into the fan and circle areas, as well as 1″ beyond the marked perimeter square.

2. Using your tracing paper shape as a template (see Before You Begin, page 115), pin piece 1 onto the muslin foundation and use clear thread to machine stitch it into place along the edges of the fabric. There's no need to stitch the center edge down, as the entire circle will be stitched later. To add the pieces around the center circle, you are using a modified version of the freezer-paper appliqué method (page 32). See the note below for more information.

3. For piece 2, press under by ¼″ the edge that will overlap piece 1. Pin this in place onto the muslin foundation and topstitch along the edge of the fold.

4. Piece 3 has a slightly curved edge to iron under, but it is gentle so you can get a smooth, turned-under curved edge. After pressing, pin it in place over piece 2 and topstitch down. Repeat with piece 4.

5. Piece 5 has 2 turned-under edges, and a corner is formed where these edges meet. Pin this piece so that the shorter turned-under edge continues along the same seamline as piece 4. Pin both sides, as shown, then sew in place and topstitch.

6. Pieces 6 and 7 are sewn on in the same manner as pieces 4 and 5 (see Steps 4 and 5).

Note

Freezer paper is not used here! This is a more free-form appliqué method, but using the same concept of ironing under the seam allowance, overlapping it onto the adjoining fabric shape, and machine appliquéing it down.

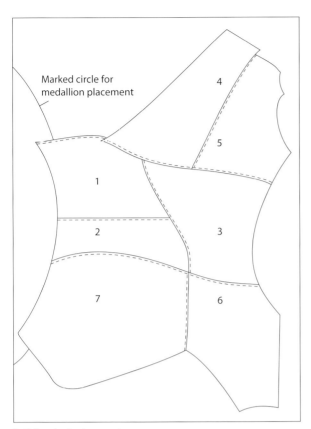

Marked circle for
medallion placement

4

5

1

3

2

7

6

Building the background

Are you getting the feel of this? Have a look to see if you can tell how this is going together.

My piecing is progressing around the circle.

Let's keep going....

Piecing continues.

We have just pieced the first ring around the center where eventually the medallion will be appliquéd onto the quilt.

AUDITIONING FABRICS AS YOU GO

At this stage, I find it helpful to just dump my fabric scraps on the floor so I can pick and choose among the bits. I pin likely fabric candidates to my quilt on the design wall to get an idea of placement and to keep things balanced. I take a digital picture to see how it looks reduced, as this often reveals a patch or area that jars because it is too dark or too large.

I like to place solid fabrics next to prints or more textured fabrics. However, we all know that some fabrics have minds of their own and will sometimes just go where they choose to go.

This kind of auditioning, pinning, and photographing works for me, and I enjoy it so much.

Continue piecing

Now we will add pieces to the first ring, using the chunk method (page 34). In the following three pictures, you can see how one of the chunks is pieced together and added.

The back of my chunked pieces, showing the seams

The front, with the edge to be appliquéd pressed under

The chunk pinned in place and partially sewn down

Continue piecing up to the edges marked for all four fans.

MAKE ADJUSTMENTS

After you complete the foundation piecing/appliquéing/chunking, you might find that some of the patch shapes bother you a little. This is easy to remedy.

1. Place a piece of tracing paper over the area you want to tweak and draw your new shape.

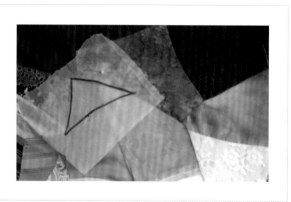

The paper template shows where my new patch will go.

2. Cut out your paper shape, adding a seam allowance, and use it to cut out the fabric you want to add. Press under the seam allowances, pin into place, and topstitch in clear thread, right over the patches already there. Once the embellishment goes over those seams, no one will know you did this. It's a trick I use all the time.

I like this curve better than the pointed piecing that was under it.

Sometimes it is important to just leave your quilt on the design wall and look at it for a day or two. After doing so, I decided to turn the whole thing a quarter of the way around! We have to stay flexible as we design. It's important not to become too attached to any one solution along the way.

At least, this is how I like to work. An equally wonderful method is to graph out in detail the entire design, both piecing and embellishment, before you even get out your fabrics. It all depends on what working process feels the most natural for *you*.

My life-changing design moment

While we are talking about design, I want to share with you a conversation that the very great art quilter Erica Carter had with me years ago. I was three days into a five-day workshop and floundering badly. I wanted to throw everything out!

Me:

What do you do when you've been working on a quilt and you get to the point where you absolutely hate it?

EC:

Oh, that's the best time! Do you know why? It is because that's when you become willing to take some risks. You have to make a leap. And that's when the breakthrough comes.

I have never forgotten this. It changed everything for me.

Now when I get to that frenzied I-hate-it stage while in the midst of a project (and it happens every time, believe me), I recognize this as normal. I calm down and even trust that state of mind. It is simply part of the process.

If this happens to you, just keep working and look for the place to take your leap. Almost always, you will land safely.

✾ Finish and Embellish the Background

When the background crazy piecing is completed to your satisfaction, zigzag stitch the edges all the way around the pieced area, as well as around the inside circle.

Completed background piecing

I chose a "formula" for my embellishments, just like I did for my piecing (which uses only shades and hues of blue). For this project, I decided to use only silk ribbon and make just a few kinds of stitches, to keep my embroidery bold and graphic. Sometimes limiting choices can make a much stronger impact than having too many different things going on at once, even in crazy quilts. (For specifics about silk ribbon embroidery, see page 44. For the stitches, see page 37.)

Shall we see if this formula works?

Simple rows of herringbone, cretan, fly, chevron, chain, or buttonhole stitches are worked in wonderful 4mm silk ribbon by River Silks (see Suppliers, page 127).

❦ Add the Medallion and Fans to the Foundation

Now it's time to put it all together. We will trim the medallion and fans to their finished sizes, appliqué them to the foundation, and add more embellishments.

Before trimming the fan and circles, add some machine echo quilting in the white ring area, if desired. Add a layer of muslin behind the medallion and fan squares, using the adhesive fabric spray or basting it into place.

I used Sulky Sliver metallic thread for my quilting. I think this little sparkly element is a nice decorative addition. Keep in mind that this is not functional quilting, though there will be a little of that later.

There is no need to mark quilting lines—just follow the outside edges of the floral elements in the fans and medallion, in lines about ⅛" apart or so, using the edge of your machine's presser foot as a guide. The quilting in the white ring should be about 2" deep, or about 10 to 14 rows.

Trim to fit

Next, trim the center medallion and the 4 corner fans so they can be appliquéd onto the pieced background. The medallion should be 21" in diameter, including the quilted white ring border.

1. Find the center of the medallion by folding its square background into quarters. Mark the center point with a pin.

2. For this application, I chose to make a tracing paper template that measures 10½" per side (see How to Measure Large Circles of Any Size, page 112). Mark the center.

3. Center the circle template by placing its center directly over the pin in the medallion's center. Pin the template into place. Mark the circumference with a water-soluble marker, remove the template, and trim the white fabric in a circle.

4. Cut away the extra layer of white ring fabric from the center of the back of the medallion by making a careful slit in it with scissors and then cutting the fabric along the edge of the quilting from the back. Leave about a ½" margin.

5. To trim the fans, cut a 21" circle template into quarters and pin each quarter over the fan squares, lining up the right-angle corners. Mark and trim the curves. Then cut away the extra white ring fabric from the center of the back, ½" from the quilting, as you did for the medallion.

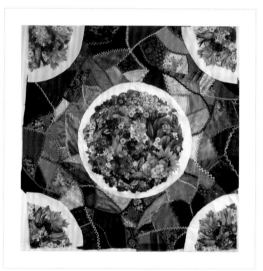

My quilted and trimmed fans and medallion, pinned on my background piecing

Appliqué to the background

1. Re-mark the finished 40″ × 40″ square on the front of the quilt. (See Tip, page 121, for my method.)

2. Make sure the medallion is centered and the fans are lined up with the finished corners of the pieced background, and then pin them into place.

3. Measure, measure, and re-measure! Confirm that your finished quilt will be 40″ × 40″.

Tip

To measure exactly, I use an unorthodox method: I place my large rotary cutting mat on top of my quilt, lining up one corner over a corner of the quilt. (Be sure your mat is clean!)

This way, I get a perfect right angle and two long, perfectly straight edges along the sides of my quilt for drawing my sewing line. I fit other large rulers into place so that my quilt's entire perimeter can be measured at once, with all four sides and corners exactly square and straight. I mark the corners with water-soluble ink at 10¼" per side, and I place my fans in these marked corners.

4. Carefully machine appliqué the medallion and fan assemblies into place, using a clear thread in a narrow zigzag stitch along their perimeter raw edges.

ADD BEADING

Now is the time to add beading to the medallion and fans! This will help attach the pieces to the pieced background while also providing embellishment (see Beads, page 39).

Gather lots of small beads. Seed beads, pressed flower beads, crystals—whatever you have on hand that would look good in the centers of all those gathered ribbon flowers. I decided to feature some sparkly crystal montée beads.

(You know, it is good to use your very favorite beads. Use them up if you have to, but use them! It will make you so happy.)

After your medallion and fans are in place, you may find you need to add an extra ribbon flower or two to balance your composition.

QUILTING

My emphatic opinion is that quilting does not belong on crazy quilts. I just don't think the addition of that kind of surface element integrates well with all the embroidery and embellishment. (Debra Jo Hardman's quilt *A Modern Romance*, page 64, is a blazing exception to this rule.)

That being said, quilting can have its functional uses. I added some free-motion machine quilting in clear thread to some of the flowers. But I only added as much as necessary to help stabilize and smooth out my medallion and fans.

The quilting also helped define some of the petals. This is a very personal call on your part. Add what quilting you think your project needs … or skip it!

Add the medallion and fan borders

Your fans and medallion are beaded and appliquéd into place, but what about their raw edges? I covered mine with ribbon embroidery, but you could use trim if you prefer. I chose 13mm silk ribbon, again by River Silks. Using a size 18 chenille needle, I made a puffy and solid line of herringbone stitches (see Classic Crazy Quilt Stitches, page 36) around all my fans and the medallion. This required approximately 25 yards of ribbon. (For details on ribbon embroidery, see page 44.)

I covered the raw edges with ribbon embroidery in a herringbone stitch.

Lace with sequins beaded into place

If you decide to add a lace border to the edges of your fans and medallion, as I did, it is a simple matter to pin and tack it into place by hand. (I used Mokuba lace #61096K.) Using lace this way gives an awful lot of interest and texture with not much work. It also allowed me to integrate the white of the rings into the pieced background, which helped unify the look of the quilt. In all, I used 4 yards of lace.

Beading some sequins into place over the flowers in the lace was my last addition to the quilt top before assembling the quilt. There are many ways to embellish lace; I chose this method because I didn't want the lace to look just plopped on. The colors of the sequins, and the overall pattern they make (though subtle), helped integrate the lace into the quilt. Also, sequins are cheap!

❧ Create the False Back

Heavily embellished crazy quilts are meant to be displayed, not used. Our goal as crazy quilters is to have our quilts hang straight and true, with the surface even and flat. We don't want wrinkles or sagging patches to distract the viewer from all the delights of our embellishment work, and we want those embellishments to stay put.

Creating a false back of muslin, which is heavily basted through a thin batting to the foundation fabric of the quilt top, provides an internal structure to support the quilt from within. I first learned this technique from Annie Whitsed, of Canberra, Australia, and I am forever grateful to her.

I prefer to use cotton drapery lining fabric for my crazy quilt batting. It can be found in fabric stores that have a home decorating department. It is usually 60" wide and is kind of spongy, like flannel but with a looser weave, so it is easy to stitch through. It is also fairly inexpensive. This woven "batting" adds more support to the quilt's interior than nonwoven quilt batting does.

However, if you have old batting scraps that you need to use up, they will work just fine, particularly in smaller quilts. I just wouldn't use anything too puffy.

1. Cut the batting and false back fabric (a lightweight muslin is best) to 44" × 44".

2. Lay the quilt top facedown, followed by the batting, and then the false back on top. Pin baste the layers together, with pins every 10".

3. Lay the quilt sandwich on a flat surface and begin basting the layers from the back, through the muslin, the batting, and into the foundation fabric of the quilt top. With each stitch, check to make sure that nothing shows on the front. (This is a pain, but it is *worth it*.) Use a small basting stitch for this, perhaps an inch long. Rows of basting should go across the quilt horizontally at 2" intervals.

Here, the false back is being basted to the batting and quilt top. (I've hung it up to show you how it looks.)

Tip

When you come to a seam between assembled blocks, pierce the seam allowances with a basting stitch. Sharon Boggon takes this technique a step further, bringing her basting needle up to the surface of her quilt, taking it through a bead or button, and then returning it to the back again. (See her beautiful quilt _Crazy Diamonds,_ page 59.) This is an especially good idea where there is a heavily weighted encrustation of embellishments.

You can also baste more closely in a circle around any area that needs extra support. Remember, these stitches will not show after the dressy back is attached over the false back.

Before you pin baste the dressy back over the false back, trim the edges of the quilt sandwich to ½" from where the finished edge will be. You don't need an extra margin now.

❧ Attach the Dressy Back

A tightly woven fabric for the dressy back will add a bit of extra stability to the quilt. It is best to avoid fabric that is too loosely woven, and velvet can be a wiggly challenge. Quilters' cotton can be a fine choice. I tend to prefer dupioni silk for that extra dash of opulence and because it is a surprisingly durable fabric.

I like to use buttons to attach the dressy back to the quilt, because they have just a bit more surface area than beads or even just plain knots. They therefore provide just that much more support for the quilt when it is hung. Buttons can be a nice design element as well. They can be sewn on securely without any knots showing. Your finished back will be 40″ × 40″, so for this quilt find 25 buttons that you like.

Prepare the back

1. Cut out a 42″ × 42″ square of the fabric of your choice; iron it well.

2. Lay the dressy back over the false back with the right side up. Smooth it into place and pin baste.

3. Mark the back so that the buttons will be 7″ apart, starting 6″ in from where the finished outer edge will be.

Tip

To make sure you are accurate without putting actual marks on your fabric, simply insert the point of a straight pin where each button will go, according to your ruler. It is very sad when you measure wrongly and make permanent marks where you shouldn't have. So do please use the pins first and then mark as you remove each pin.

Attach the buttons

1. Remove the straight pin after marking the hole with a tiny dot.

2. Thread a needle with quilting or sewing machine thread, double it, and knot. Clip off any extra thread below the knot.

3. Insert the needle right next to the dot, go through all the fabric layers except the fancy fabric top layer, and make a small stitch, pulling until the knot is secured against the fabric.

4. Thread on your button, coming up through the bottom, over its top, and back through another hole. Take another stitch into the quilt under the button (checking again to make sure you don't go all the way through to the front), pulling the button snug to the back of the quilt. Repeat (I go through each set of holes 3 times). Wrap the thread around beneath the button 3 times, creating a kind of shank, and pull it snug.

5. To knot off, take a small stitch beneath the button, wrap the thread around the tip of the needle twice, and then pull the needle through, as in a French knot, holding down the wrapped thread with your thumb as you pull. This knot should not be visible.

6. Take another small stitch to bury the thread, come up, and snip off at the surface of the fabric.

You can develop a nice rhythm doing this, and the buttons will all be attached in no time.

Buttons, firmly sewn on the dressy back

❧ Finish Your Quilt

You are nearly finished! The final steps of trimming, binding, and labeling your quilt are all that remain.

Square up

Now is the time to re-measure the edges of your quilt and trim them exactly to size.

One reason I wait to do this until now is that I don't want to accidentally cut off the ends of any of my embroidered seams. Another reason is that I want all my layers—the top, batting, and false and dressy backs—securely in place before I square up my quilt.

Re-measure your quilt's perimeter to make sure that all is square and that the sides are of equal lengths. Once again, mark the finished perimeter all the way around. This new line may coincide with the previous marking. Occasionally the new line is more accurate due to distortion caused by sewing.

Sew over the newly marked line all the way around the quilt with a narrow zigzag stitch. Then and only then, when you have made sure there are no wrinkles in the dressy back formed by this stitching, carefully trim the edges ¼" from the sewing line.

This perimeter machine zigzag stitching, which further stabilizes the quilt, will be covered by the quilt binding.

Add a binding

For this quilt, I used 1½"-wide wired ribbon to bind the edges. It is a simple task to pin one edge of the ribbon to the quilt front just past the sewing line, and then to fold the ribbon and pin the other edge to the back. Shape the miters at the corners and pin them into place.

I prefer the greater control I get from stitching this down by hand, rather than by machine. It is good to hand sew the miters closed as well.

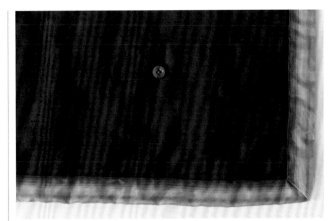

My wire-edged ribbon binding, shown on the dressy silk back

I pinned and then whipstitched a final row of rickrack trim in place on the front along the edge of the wired ribbon binding. The thin line of a darker value added just a little more decorative definition. As you can see, in crazy quilting we make design decisions until the very last!

I added decoratively woven rickrack trim on the quilt front.

Sign the front of your quilt, either with permanent ink or an embroidered signature. A label on the back, including your name, the quilt's name, the date, and the place of origin, is the final touch on your masterpiece!

In Conclusion

Summer Departs, 13″ × 13″, by the author, 2008

Whether your are sewing with friends or spending those golden hours stitching alone with your thoughts, crazy quilting is a vehicle for lovely inner experiences.

Whether you choose to follow in the proud steps of tradition or to launch into fearless experimentation, practicing the disciplines of crazy quilting will enhance your artistry.

Creating, stitching, playing, reflecting, and loving the endless possibilities ... we engage all these faculties when we crazy quilt. We learn to listen to our work and it tells us where to go, which is so deeply satisfying.

And, we can tell stories.

My hope is that this book will help you stitch wonderful stories of your own.

—Allie

Suppliers

I offer my special thanks to the fine suppliers listed below, whose products have enhanced my work in this book. Visit their websites to find out where to buy their beautiful and helpful products.

C&T Publishing
for TAP (Transfer Artist Paper) and fast2fuse interfacing
www.ctpub.com

The Electric Quilt Company
for the best prepared fabric sheets for inkjet printing
www.electricquilt.com

Kreinik Thread
for metallic threads
www.kreinik.com

Mokuba
for beautiful lace (see materials for *Crazy Happy Flowers*, page 111) and beautiful ribbon
www.mokubany.com

River Silks
for the best-quality silk ribbon
www.riversilks.com

Thai Silks
for beautiful silk packs
www.thaisilks.com

Walnut Hollow
for the Creative Textile Tool
www.walnuthollow.com

The Warm Company
for Steam-A-Seam fusible tape and Beads-2-Fuse
www.warmcompany.com

Other fine online purveyors of all kinds of wonderful crazy quilt supplies:

Ally's Bazaar
for deeply discounted jacquard ribbon
www.allysbazaar.com

Colors of Rengin
for Turkish oya flowers (see page 115)
www.artfire.com/users/colorsofrengin

Creative Stitchery Success Strips
www.embroiderysuccess-strips.com

Evening Star Designs
for Carole Samples Dream-A-Seam templates
www.eveningstardesigns.citymax.com

Lacis
for stamped brass bees (see detail of *Crazy Happy Flowers*, page 115)
www.lacis.com

Maureen's Vintage Acquisitions
www.maureensvintageacquisitions.com

The Pink Bunny
www.valeriebothell.com

Ribbonsmyth
www.ribbonsmyth.com

Vintage Vogue
www.vintagevogue.com

About the Author

Photo by Robert Allen

Allie Aller has been a fiber girl all her life. She was a "sane quilter" for twenty years, but crazy quilting took over her life in 2001 and has since brought her immense joy. She lives in the country at the mouth of the beautiful Columbia River Gorge in Washougal, Washington, with her gardening husband, Robert. They have two grown sons.

Visit her blog: alliesinstitches.blogspot.com

Great Titles *from* C&T PUBLISHING & STASH BOOKS

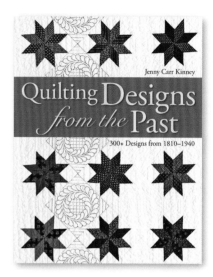

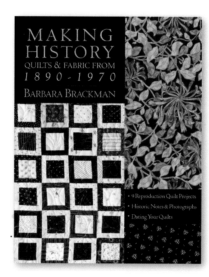

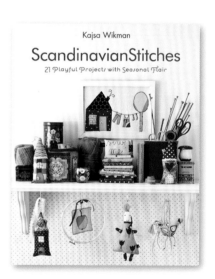

Available at your local retailer or **www.ctpub.com** *or* **800-284-1114**

For a list of other fine books from C&T Publishing, visit our website to view our catalog online.

C&T PUBLISHING, INC.

P.O. Box 1456
Lafayette, CA 94549
800-284-1114

Email: ctinfo@ctpub.com
Website: www.ctpub.com

C&T Publishing's professional photography services are now available to the public. Visit us at www.ctmediaservices.com.

Tips and Techniques can be found at www.ctpub.com > Consumer Resources > Quiltmaking Basics: Tips & Techniques for Quiltmaking & More

For quilting supplies:

COTTON PATCH

1025 Brown Ave.
Lafayette, CA 94549
Store: 925-284-1177
Mail order: 925-283-7883

Email: CottonPa@aol.com
Website: www.quiltusa.com

Note: Fabrics used in the quilts shown may not be currently available, as fabric manufacturers keep most fabrics in print for only a short time.